W9-DGT-216

KEY ISSUES IN EDUCATION —
COMPARATIVE PERSPECTIVES

or

They do it Differently Abroad

KEY ISSUES IN EDUCATION

Comparative Perspectives

Edited by
KEITH WATSON

CROOM HELM
London • Sydney • Dover, New Hampshire

Introduction, Chapters 5 & 7 © 1985 K. Watson. Chapter 3 © 1985
Edmund King. Chapter I © 1985 Patricia Broadfoot. Chapter 2 © 1985.
W.D. Halls. Chapter 4 © 1985 Margaret Sutherland. Chapter 6 © 1985 Derek Esp.

Croom Helm Ltd, Provident House, Burrell Row,
Beckenham, Kent BR3 1AT

Croom Helm Australia Pty Ltd, Suite 4, 6th Floor,
64-76 Kippax Street, Surry Hills, NSW 2010, Australia

British Library Cataloguing in Publication Data.

Key issues in education: comparative perspectives,
    or, They do it differently abroad.
    1. Comparative education
    I. Watson, Keith, 1939-
370.19'5   LA133

ISBN 0-7099-2795-9

Croom Helm, 51 Washington Street, Dover,
New Hampshire 03820, USA

Library of Congress Cataloging in Publication Data
Main entry under title:

Key issues in education – comparative perspectives, or,
    They do it differently abroad.

    1. Education – Great Britain – Addresses, essays,
lectures. 2. Education – Europe – Addresses, essays,
lectures. 3. Comparative education – Addresses,
essays, lectures. I. Watson, Keith.
LA632.K45   1985   370.19'5   85-14961
ISBN 0-7099-2795-9

Word processing and layout by
Christine Computers, Northampton
Printed and bound in Great Britain by
Biddles Ltd, Guildford and King's Lynn

DISCARDED
WIDENER UNIVERSITY

WIDENER UNIVERSITY
WOLFGRAM
LIBRARY
CHESTER, PA.

CONTENTS

LIST OF CONTRIBUTORS

PATRICIA BROADFOOT   is a Lecturer in Education at Bristol
                           University School of Education.

DEREK ESP   is Deputy Education Officer for
                           Somerset County Council.

W.D. HALLS   is Senior Tutor in the University of
                           Oxford and in the Department of
                           Educational Studies, Oxford.

EDMUND KING   is Emeritus Professor of Education at
                           King's College, University of London.

MARGARET SUTHERLAND   is Professor of Education at the
                           University of Leeds.

KEITH WATSON   is a Lecturer in Education at the
                           University of Reading School of
                           Education.

INTRODUCTION - "THEY DO IT DIFFERENTLY ABROAD"

Keith Watson

Soon after he was appointed Secretary of State for Education and Science Sir Keith Joseph was reported on several occasions as saying: "I keep asking my civil servants 'Do they do it better abroad? I suspect they do......'" We were never told what the civil servants replied, even if they knew, but there was an implication in these comments that, although other countries might arrange their educational provision differently from our own, they might tackle certain of the issues better than ourselves and as a result there was something that could be learnt from a study of comparative education.

It has been part of the stock-in-trade of comparative educationists since the time of Marc-Antoine Jullien in the early nineteenth century that by looking at educational developments in other societies not only can we better understand our own educational system, but that we can also learn, borrow ideas and even introduce reforms. The apparent keenness of the Secretary of State for comparative studies was, therefore, to be welcomed. While there is some evidence that members of the Department of Education and Science have begun to take seriously some aspects of comparative education, most notably in their recognition of the need to train headteachers, to lay down guidelines for a core curriculum of knowledge and subjects to be studied and the introduction of pupil profiles as part of their overall assessment, there is increasing evidence to show that in teacher preparation, whether at pre-service or in-service levels, the comparative aspects of education have been downgraded in favour of more functional classroom management skills and techniques.(1) (Watson, 1982, 1985).

It was concern that too many local education authority teachers were ethnocentric, were bogged down with their own school and classroom problems and were often totally unaware of what might be occurring in schools and classrooms in other parts of the world, that led to a decision to hold a series of public lectures in the University of Reading School of Education during 1983 under the general heading of "They Do It

2

Differently Abroad - a comparative perspective on some contemporary issues". It was generally recognised that many of the problems faced by teachers in English schools - curriculum innovation, multicultural provision, classroom discipline, examination reform - are not dissimilar from those faced by teachers in other industrialised nations of the world. Indeed the similarities in the problems are striking: it is in how these problems are resolved that the differences arise.

All the contributors to the lecture series, on which this volume of essays is based, not only have an expertise in comparative education as well as in certain specific facets of education which they have studied from a comparative perspective, but they all believe passionately that we should learn from developments that are taking place in other countries. Certain aspects of English education might be deemed to be successful, e.g. primary education, the numbers of working-class children reaching university, the efficiency of universities in producing graduates in three years, etc., but set into a broader international context much of what is taken for granted and is assumed to be efficient, e.g. the examination structure or our flexible decentralized control of education, may in fact be remarkably inefficient and this country may actually be well down in the league table of educational success, as Sir Keith Joseph implied.

The following pages, therefore, are written in an attempt to help teachers, students, politicians, administrators and members of the lay public to look critically at certain key issues in contemporary education and try to set the English context into a wider international perspective and more particularly a Western European one. Undoubtedly one of the most burning issues of the English educational scene is that of examination reform, especially in the light of Sir Keith Joseph´s announcement in June 1984 that a new system of examinations for sixteen-year-olds is to be introduced in 1986, and the belief, shared by many, that formal external examinations at that age will have been abandoned by the 1990s. The best form of assessing, examining and selecting pupils is part of the ongoing debate about education. Every twenty years or so in England there appears to be a major readjustment in the examination structures. Other societies, most notably China, experiment with complete abolition and alternative forms of assessment and selection, but even there after a decade of abolition (1966-76) formal examinations have been reintroduced. Countries nearer home, such as Denmark and Sweden, while formally abolishing school leaving examinations, have nevertheless worked out a complex system of internal continuous assessment.

As Patricia Broadfoot shows in her chapter on examination reforms, not only are public examinations "a peculiarly English disease" but England is very much out of step with other European countries over the question of examinations. After looking at the purpose and role of examinations and other forms of assessment Patricia Broadfoot discusses some of the ongoing reforms that have either been proposed or are being introduced elsewhere in Europe, including profiles and continuous assessment. She stresses the need to think afresh the best forms of assessment for different types of pupil, especially in the light of changing employment patterns. One is left wondering not only whether there is a long way to go in reforming the English examination structures but whether or not the decision formally to examine at 16+ is still necessary.

A second key issue, and perhaps the most persistent of all - educational reform theories and objectives since the Second World War - certainly one that has outlived all the many more short-lived fads - is that of equality of educational opportunity for all children, or, as the French like to call it, the democratisation of education. W.D. Halls, one of the foremost authorities in this field, explores this issue in the context of Western Europe. His conclusions can make none of us feel complacent. In spite of all the rhetoric from politicians and educationists alike not only is England very far from the ideal of equality of opportunity but she compares unfavourably with most of her European counterparts in this particular area. As Halls points, out the lack of any central co-ordinated planning, the devolution of powers to local education authorities, the confusing range and variety of the English school system, the lack of a common curriculum, together with early specialisation for a few and the presence of a substantial number of private and prestigious institutions all hamper moves towards equality of opportunity and, if anything, lead to greater inequality. The implications of the argument and that there needs to be some fundamental rethinking about the purposes and the processes of education in England and Wales.

The area where the greatest confusion and uncertainty exist is also the very one where the greatest pressures exist, namely that of post-compulsory provision for the 16 to 19-year-olds. Here again, as Edmund King so admirably shows, Britain lags far behind other industrialised countries. Not only are there pressures on individual teenagers in the form of peer group pressures, job uncertainties and the emotional changes as adolescents become young adults, but there is uncertainty in the highest quarters about how this age range should best be prepared for living in a rapidly changing society and in a rapidly changing job market. The variety of provision in England, the lack of any co-ordinated planning, the uncertainty about whether members of the 16 to 19 age range should be treated as children/teenagers or as young adults, all clearly set England apart from her neighbours. Edmund King's cry for greater co-ordination and for the need to learn from other societies should be heeded.

The question of curriculum control, central direction and

uniform structure - or lack of it - also occurs in Margaret Sutherland's analysis os sex bias in education. Once again England is shown to be falling behind in attempts to provide greater equality of opportunity for the female sex. She argues that co-educational comprehensive education can actually hinder the education of girls in certain subject areas because stereotyping becomes more acute than in single-sex institutions, unless, as in the case of much of Europe, there is far greater control of what is studied in the curriculum and there are far fewer choices until a later stage of schooling. Unfortunately the teachers' unions and the professional organisations in England have shown a reluctance to accept greater central direction and more uniform control of the curriculum. Her conclusion that we ought to consider "whether the very flexibility of our educational system allows stereotype to persist where more resolute centralised policies in other systems may at least be getting rid of some of them.." should give much food for thought.

One of the most striking developments to have changed the classrooms of many cities in Europe in the epast twenty years has been the influx of large numbers of migrant workers' children or the immigrant children from non-European backgrounds. Many teachers in the UK have developed a siege mentality, believing that they alone have been left to cope with the iniquities of the system. Keith Watson's study of developments in Western Europe shows that this is not only not the case, but that where positive policies have been pursued at national level there has been considerable progress. There is much that British teachers in multicultural classrooms can learn by studying how other teachers in other schools across Europe are coping with one of the most fundamental educational and social issues of the 1980s.

Whatever aspect of education one considers, without clear leadership and direction, reforms are liable to falter. It has been widely acknowledged for some years now that, of all the industrialised nations of the world, Britain has lagged behind in the training of the headteachers and deputies. Whereas it is impossible to get a headship in the USA or Canada or even in France without first having had some kind of training and preparation, the pattern in the UK has been for heads to "learn on the job". As Derek Esp, one of the pioneers in this field in this country, argues, this approach is no longer acceptable. He shows how headteachers are trained, selected and prepared in a variety of European settings. There is no one way - the variety shows that - but what Esp is urging is for all heads and deputies to be trained for a school system that is rapidly changing and that is responding to an increasing number of pressures from society. Since Esp undertook his first survey in Europe in 1980 the Department of Education and Science in England has recognised the need for training for headship. This in itself is a positive argument in favour of comparative studies since officials were convinced by the wealth of information from other societies.

The last of the key issues analysed in this volume may appear to be a strange one, but the furor that has surrounded the question of corporal punishment in English schools warranted its inclusion. Keith Watson looks at the many and varying arguments for and against corporal punishment in schools and the moves towards abolition and shows how and why England and Wales are now so out of step with their European neighbours including Eire and Scotland. In so doing he highlights some quite fundamental differences in attitude towards education and schooling between the English teachers and their European counterparts, and while not condoning corporal punishment he urges a more fundamental look at the wider issues before introducing abolition legislation overnight.

It is recognised that these are only a few of the many contemporary educational issues that could have been explored comparatively. It is hoped, however, that even by taking these seven issues - examination reform, democratisation, 16-19 provison, sex bias, multicultural provision, training for headship and corporal punishment - readers will wish to explore others in greater detail and will appreciate that by looking at educational issues cross-nationally much can be learnt which is of practical, as opposed to theoretical, value. Thus while other countries may or may not do things better than ourselves in educational provision, practice and policy they do "do it differently".

NOTES AND REFERENCES

1.Watson,K. (1982): Comparative Education in British Teacher Education in Goodings,R., Byram,M. and McPartland,M. (eds): Changing Priorities in Teacher Education, Croom Helm, London.

Watson,K. and Williams,P.R.C. (1985): Comparative Studies and International Awareness in Teacher Education, Journal of Education of Teachers, (forthcoming, January 1985).

Chapter One

COMPARATIVE PERSPECTIVES ON THE REFORM OF EXAMINATIONS

Patricia Broadfoot

The inspiration and title for this series of papers comes from a remark made by Sir Keith Joseph and reported in the Times of the 18th November 1982, in which he suggested that other countries organised their educational provision differently from our own. The implication of what was said is that some of these different practices may also be better practices and that we could do well to inform ourselves of what is going on in countries facing very similar educational problems to those faced by England at the present time. Such a willingness to learn is particularly necessary in the field of assessment and examinations since it is not generally appreciated in this country how far out of line England is in examination practice as compared with the rest of the western world. Although most industrialised countries still retain some bestiges of public examinations, the scale of the enterprise in England is very much greater than elsewhere, to the extent that it may be said that public examinations are a peculiarly English disease. This, of course, prompts the question why examinations should figure so prominently in English education in contrast to what is done abroad and, associated with this, whether we have anything to learn from the practices of these other countries in our attempts to reform our examination system.

Clearly there is widespread recognition in England at the present time that all is not well with existing practice. There is much talk of reform, the replacement of GCE "O" level and CSE (the Certificate of Secondary Education) by a common system of examining at 16+,* a possible 17+ Certificate of Pre-vocational Education (CPVE), the institution of profiles for all 16-year-olds and various kinds of qualifications for the expanding further education sector of the education system. Add to this the more specialist concerns of, for example, the new Secondary Examinations Council, which, according to its chairman, Sir Wilfred Cockcroft, will take as its first concern the intensive scrutiny of the GCE Advanced Level examination(1) and the detailed research currently being pursued by the

Schools Council and others on the potential of graded tests, non-cognitive assessment, oral assessment and other novel initiatives, and it is clear that there is a considerable amount of effort being applied to developing and improving the existing system of examinations in this country. The main reasons for these attempts at reform are the major changes currently taking place in the relationship between schooling and employment. Not only has the advent of widespread youth unemployment brought about a radical change in post-16 educational provision in the so-called VIth, it has also brought about a heavy investment in non-traditional forms of vocational training sponsored by the Department of Industry and the Department of Employment, notably in the latter case, through the Manpower Services Commission and the Youth Training Scheme. Indeed it would be fair to say that it is the rapidly expanding non-traditional part of the education system, as found in various forms of further education, which is leading current initiatives in providing new forms of examination, simply because it is in these areas particularly that the shortcomings of traditional certification and selection procedures are so clearly evident as not to be gainsaid.

Given that there is such widespread recognition at the present time of the need for reform, plus a not inconsiderable amount of development work apparently going on, what, if anything, can be usefully learned from "how they do it abroad"? In order to answer this question it is necessary first to clarify in rather more detail what we mean by examinations and the various functions they perform in contemporary society. First of all a definition. William Solberg in _Ottobre_ (1979) defines an examination as "a more or less formalised procedure usually separated from the classroom situation". (One refers to candidates rather than pupils). "The candidate who passes the examination is awarded a certificate or diploma which gives him some rights including the right to be admitted to higher types of education." Thus, whilst educational _assessment_ can be both formative, that is during the course of education, and summative, marking the end of a stage of education, _examinations_ are normally concerned with summative assessment. More specifically examinations relate to the three different functions of _certification_, attesting to be the attainment of a particular standard, _prediction_ of probable future performance and _evaluation_ in more general terms of the overall standard of a group of pupils - a standard which is often taken to be the basis of educational accountability. It is this last function which is of critical importance in maintaining the domination of examinations in English education. Whilst other countries need some form of assessment to attest to what pupils have achieved and as the basis for occupational allocation, it is England´s peculiarly decentralised curriculum provision which makes public examinations of such particular importance in perpetuating a measure of standardised curriculum control. (Broadfoot, 1979).

Thus, for more than a hundred years, since the advent of mass education itself, examinations have provided an extremely effective and convenient basis for selection and system control. Yet the arguments against them are equally long-standing, reaching a new peak at the present time. (Satterly, 1981). These include criticisms that examinations are socially biased in favour of middle-class pupils, that they are inaccurate and have a poor predictive power, that they emphasise a passive and over-academic approach to learning, that they produce an obsessive degree of tension and anxiety amongst candidates and, not least, that they are extremely expensive. (Ingenkamp, 1977). These arguments are well illustrated by a country such as Japan which, even more than England, is dominated by examinations at every level of the education system to the extent that Japan may be called a "degreeocracy" and where for many children life is dominated by the phenomenon of preparing for and often endlessly repeating one examination after another, since typically this is the only way into a particular occupation or social status. The high level of adolescent disturbance and indeed suicide associated with this practice is sufficient testimony to one of the major disadvantages of examinations. (Shimahara, 1979).

On the other hand, proponents of public examinations argue that they fulfil the need among young people for ritual and for competition, that they help to maintain motivation, that they underpin standards, that they are the only fair basis for occupational selection and that they help justify the inevitable inequalities in a competitive society. In considering the reform of examinations it is important to bear both sets of arguments in mind. Examinations are almost inevitably elitist. Designed to allow the identification and selection of the best available talent, they cannot but restrict the educational opportunities of the rest, who are thereby labelled failures. Yet they are also one of the principal bastions of egalitarianism in providing for equality of opportunity and a much fairer basis for selection than that of family wealth and nepotism which they have typically replaced. Thus the reform of examinations must have at its centre the desire to maintain the widest possible degree of opportunity for all pupils without sacrificing the nation's ability to identify and recruit talent in the most profitable way.

One way in which examinations are clearly not being used in the most efficient manner is where countries continue with an examination system designed for a time in which secondary schooling was for a select minority. Secondary education is compulsory in all developed countries - typically up to the age of 16 - and more and more young people are staying on to 18 and beyond. Increasingly too it is the norm for such compulsory secondary education to be comprehensive in some countries, such as Sweden or the USA, even up to the age of 18. Ten or twenty years ago the norm in Europe at least was selection at the end of elementary or primary school around the age of 11. Thus, for example, in the Netherlands during the 1960s, children would be selected for high school, technical vocational school or general secondary school; in Spain, before 1970, they would be selected at 10+ for high school or higher elementary school, and in France, similarly, there was a tripartite selection between general, technical and high school education at around the age of 11. In most European countries, with the notable exception of West Germany, such 11+ selection by examination has now given way to either comprehensive secondary education or, where there are still different kinds of secondary provision, selection on a different basis to that of formal examinations. Both sorts of procedure are to be found in England where for the minority there is still selection at 11+ but where this selection is typically based on some kind of continuous assessment or aptitude test rather than the traditional formal examination.

Just as in most countries there used to be selection for different kinds of secondary school, so there was also some form of certification at around the age of 16 for that minority of children selected for the more academic high school. Thus the old lower school certificate established in England in 1917 and replaced in 1951 by "O" levels was matched in West Germany by the Mittlere Reife, the Brevet d'Etudes du Premier Cycle in France, the Certificate of Elementary Education in Spain and the Slutbetyg in Sweden. As these qualifications have become the finishing point for mass compulsory education rather than a stage in the careers of already selected pupils as hitherto, the formal examinations on which they were once based have given way to some form of continuous assessment by teachers, or, in some cases, such as New Zealand, a modified form of teacher assessment based on school accreditation.

England is the exception to this pattern. The brief popularity of Mode III, teacher-designed and assessed 16+ certificates during the 1960s for both CSE and GCE is now being rapidly eroded in favour of a return to formal, externally set and marked public examinations. This trend towards the use of teacher assessments and, in some places, standardised tests for certification at the end of compulsory schooling, may be understood as part of a process of qualification inflation. (Dore, 1976). That is to say, as more and more children are staying on at school, the significance of the 16+ certificate becomes devalued as it becomes ever more widely available. This diminution of the certificate's value for selection purposes means that the process of assessment need no longer be surrounded with the elaborate ritual and anonymity of the formal, public examination, which helped to protect teachers from undue pressure when there was a great deal at stake. This trend is strengthened by the moral and practical argument that if all children are in school up to a certain stage there must be a worthwhile and attainable goal for them to work towards. The character of such an assessment goal must inevitably be descriptive rather than selective and this changing emphasis is indeed reflected in the approach to mass certification at the present time. Whereas hitherto the emphasis in formal examinations has inevitably been on that which can be assessed in written form, the move to teacher-based assessment also allows the extension of the content of certification to include novel areas such as attitudes, skills and even personality characteristics. Typically the aim is to make a more comprehensive assessment of the individual, emphasising his or her positive qualities and giving information on those characteristics of particular interest to employers, such as punctuality, reliability and basic skills. (SCRE, 1977). Thus, for example, the French "orientation" procedure is based on a cumulative dossier of information built up, while the child goes through school, to provide a detailed basis for career and vocational guidance. This procedure is now coming to replace formal examinations in France below the level of the university matriculation examination, the Baccalaureat.

If we look at examination practice in those countries with whom we have most in common, namely those of Europe, we find that the trends I have identified are widespread and typically much further advanced than they are in England. In the Netherlands, for example, we find that the selective examination for secondary schools has been replaced by an Admissions Committee, composed of the school's governing authority, the school's principal and some teachers, who make a decision based on the report of the head of the primary school. In other countries where there is still selective secondary education, such as West Germany, we also find that examinations have been replaced by selection based on teacher assessment, followed by a common orientation stage in the fifth and sixth classes which decides, again on the basis of class tests, whether the pupil has truly been allocated to the appropriate secondary school. This spirit of positive guidance continues in Germany as it does in France with a continuous monitoring of the pupil's progress. In Italy, too, the traditionally elaborate system of teacher grades and annual promotion in the elementary and intermediate (11-14) schools has been abolished and replaced by an assessment card providing an "analytical and rounded assessment for each pupil" (Elvin, 1981), which is also the basis for school reports. Italy is perhaps unusual in still setting a final examination as early as age 14 after 3 years in the intermediate school for the Intermediate School Leaving Certificate and access to higher secondary education to which about three quarters of the age cohort proceeds. The Netherlands are marginally further along this path in that, whilst still setting an entrance examination for the higher secondary schools providing pre-university education, such examinations are combined with the results of psychological tests and continuous assessment of the last year's school work for the final decision to be made. The picture is similar also in Belgium where the Certificate of Lower Secondary Education is increasingly being awarded on the basis of continuous assessment with only borderline candidates now sitting for a formal examination.

But it is to Scandinavia that we must look for the development of this trend. As Orring (1979) suggests there is explicit recognition, in Sweden at least, that mass primary and secondary education requires a very different ethos for the education system than it did when it was basically geared to university selection if the university is not to determine the curriculum right down to the level of the lower primary school. The change required, he suggests, is an orientation in favour of getting all pupils above an "educational breadline" that is, providing minimum competency in, for example, reading. Thus as early as 1962 Sweden passed an Education Act which abolished pass/fail assessment in favour of 1-5 grading on voluntary, national, standardised achievement tests in Swedish, a foreign language and mathematics. Although voluntary these tests are taken by nearly all pupils. After 1966 similar tests were instituted for upper secondary education as well, so that now not only are pupils freed from the pressures and injustices of formal examinations but schools too are freed from the imposition of examination curricula by higher education institutions and are consequently free to determine their own priorities. Since 1970 the change has been even more radical with no matriculation qualifications for higher education entrance being required. Instead, all students completing upper secondary school now receive a leaving certificate showing the subjects taken and the marks given by the teachers. Not even the standardised test result is shown, since these are incorporated into the teachers' assessments based on all three years of the upper secondary course.

The reality for the individual student is rather less Utopian than this description would suggest however. For though no-one formally fails, students nevertheless know quite early on what kind of mark they will get, as do their teachers. Thus although there is nominally a free choice between the 23 curricula "lines" - vocational and academic - of upper secondary school, only about 60% of pupils can get their first choice for practical reasons. The rest must take their second or third choice, their power to choose depending on their results as shown on the Elementary School Leaving Certificate. In the same way, although school leaving examinations have been abolished between upper secondary and university education, there is a numerus clausus procedure operating for some of the most popular higher education subjects, entry to which again depends on marks reported on the school leaving certificate.

Indeed, throughout Europe the traditional policy of open

admission to higher education for those with matriculation in, for example, Austria, Switzerland, Belgium, Italy, West Germany and France, though never in England, is now being modified in many countries by the imposition of a numerus clausus which restricts entry to the most popular faculties. Even more significant is the growing tendency for such selection to be based not, as hitherto, on formal examination ratings, but on teachers´ marks awarded during the last years of secondary schooling. The relative decline in the importance of such traditionally prestigious examinations as the Baccalauréat in France and the Abitur in Germany can be explained as part of a much broader change in approach currently overtaking educational assessment, in which "one-off" selection is tending to be replaced by a continuing guidance process. Pupils are counselled to take the subject and later, career options, for which their day-to-day school progress seems best to fit them. This trend for formal selective examinations to be replaced by a gradual "cooling out" process (Clark, 1982) has the advantage of preventing the build-up of frustration and criticism of examination procedures, whilst still providing for the necessary process of allocating pupils to different levels of the occupational hierarchy. (Broadfoot, 1983).

In many countries the attempt to move from selective and matriculation examinations towards descriptive school-leaving certificates and, associated with this, a more explicit link between general education and vocational training, has produced major problems. These problems are particularly clear in Eastern Europe where attempts to match educational provision against anticipated manpower needs is resulting in considerable tension at the interface between school and higher education. (Mitter, 1979a). In countries such as Rumania, Poland and Bulgaria, Mitter suggests, there is a strict numerus clausus operating for the allocation of places in higher education and consequently large numbers of qualified students are unable to find a place. In the USSR up to 50% of aspiring students are frustrated in their attempts to enter higher education, at the same time lacking any more vocational qualification. It is not hard to see that, whether in a free market system of educational take-up and provision as in Western Europe or in the more planned educational provision of socialist Eastern Europe, it is highly desirable that the massive increase in application for formal higher education resulting from the opening up of secondary education be significantly reduced in favour of different forms of vocational training or, indeed, preparation for leisure, if a dangerously high level of frustration is to be avoided.

The advantages of moving from selective examinations to descriptive assessment in helping to "cool out" aspiring higher education students even for higher education are reinforced by the findings of, for example, Mitter (1979b) which suggests that, in the majority of the countries he studied, school marks

13

on secondary school leaving certificates were found to be the most reliable predictors of success at university and more useful than scholastic aptitude tests, achievement tests, interviews or indeed lotteries which, whilst being formally fair, lack public acceptability in the places where they have been tried, such as the Netherlands. Mitter also found that counselling and work experience could both contribute significantly to producing highly predictive school assessment.

To what extent, then, do they "do it differently abroad"? I have said little about practices in the United States, in Australia or other developed nations or about countries at the other end of the development scale in the Third World. I have suggested elsewhere, however, (Broadfoot, 1982) that the particular assessment policies of individual countries will be a reflection of the stage of development reached, combined with the particular institutional traditions, policy priorities and resources characteristic of that particular country. Despite their very different stage of development, Third World countries are still identifiably on the same continuum of examination practice as the developed world, albeit at an earlier stage. Thus, since most Third World countries are still at the stage of developing mass primary rather than secondary education, they typically have their key point of selection at 11+, that is, at the end of primary school. Since secondary education is still normally highly selective in such countries, there is still little pressure for reform of the necessarily formal examinations upon which such selection is based. The anonymity of public examinations is crucial in this respect. Any alternative would be likely to expose teachers to quite intolerable pressures in the need to select the favoured few from a very large number of aspiring and subsequently frustrated candidates.

In the developed world, however, despite the very different institutional traditions in, for example, Eastern and Western Europe, North America and Australia, these differences are less important than the powerful and common pressures resulting from the combination of a changing employment structure and the emergence of a powerful ideology of educational equality. Most current reforms in public examinations policy in this country and abroad can be understood as attempts to respond to the pressures I have identified. England seems to be finding it harder to come to terms with these pressures than many of the other countries that I have mentioned, although there are signs of a movement towards more descriptive teacher-based assessments, particularly at the end of compulsory schooling where there is widespread support for some kind of profile to be given to school leavers. (Balogh, 1982). There is also a powerful lobby in favour of retaining and indeed strengthening traditional pass/fail certificate examinations. (Whitty, 1983).(2) Whether a common system of examining at 16+ does indeed replace the current "O" level and CSE provision - and, although there is ministerial and professional approval for this, there are many detailed problems that need to be resolved - there is little doubt that there will continue to be a formal public examination at this stage for some considerable time, and indeed the debate with regard to Advanced Level has hardly started in this country.

It does seem to be the case that the more centralised education systems are finding it a great deal easier to minimise the role of public examinations. Thus countries such as Sweden and France are much further along the road than England or West Germany. The importance of various forms of public assessment for providing a measure of educational control is testified to by the recent accountability movement which has been much more in evidence in such decentralised countries and has served to reinforce the role of examinations and other kinds of mass testing, not only for selection purposes but as an indicator of national standards. Thus the final question that must be asked in considering how other countries have reformed examinations concerns how such countries maintain standards. The answer would seem to lie in some combination of the traditional procedures of teacher inspection and central curriculum provision combined with the more novel practice of using nationally standardised achievement tests. Such tests, like those used in Sweden, can both show whether the knowledge and skill level being achieved in different schools and regions are equal and give each teacher an idea of the class standards he should be aiming for. At the same time such tests can contribute towards the marks of an individual pupil and so provide a measure of assessment moderation between teachers and schools. More decentralised countries like England or the United States have gone some way along this path in the use of standardised tests for the monitoring of national standards, but in the United States, through the activities of the National Assessment of Educational Progress, (NAEP), and in England, through the Assessment of Performance Unit, they have so far stopped short of blanket testing in favour of light sampling, which does not allow the identification of standards for individual pupils or schools and so cannot be used in this way.

Given the dual and sometimes contradictory role that public examinations play in such decentralised countries in, on the one hand, providing for selection of individual pupils and, on the other, exerting a measure of external control over the the content and standard of what is taught, it seems likely that no major reform can be envisaged that does not provide in one way or another for both these functions to be maintained. Thus progress towards the abolition of public examinations in favour of teacher-based descriptive records is likely to be slow in England until some alternative means of measuring and control of standards nationally can be found. Learning how "they do it differently abroad" can provide valuable insights as to how this might be done. However, it is a first premise of comparative educational studies that educational policies and practices cannot be exported per se from one country to another. It is clear that England is a long way from being ready to accept alternative forms of educational control of public examinations to those accepted as traditional in this country. Thus, although pressure for change in this respect is likely to increase as schools find ever greater difficulties in motivating their pupils to work towards increasingly devalued qualifications and non-existent jobs, it is likely to be some considerable time before England is ready to take even tentative stemps towards the abolishing of public examinations.

How significant this reluctance is likely to be is a third and final question which may usefully be examined in the light of experience abroad. Such experience suggests that, whether the vehicle be formal examinations or teacher assessments, the selection function of education continues. The replacement of the "one-off" examination by an apparently more positive and benign guidance procedure over a number of years culminating in a descriptive assessment can arguably work as much against as for the interests of pupils, in that they may be labelled and categorised early in their school careers and thereafter they may be powerless to change their orientation once committed to a particular path. Real examination reform would detach the work of schools from the social need to allocate individuals to opportunities in society at large. Such reform does not yet figure in policy debates in this or in other countries for that matter. Perhaps after all England can become the hare rather than the tortoise in the reform race by giving a lead in establishing on the policy agenda such fundamental questions about the continuing desirability of linking school and society by means of any form of educational assessment.

NOTES

1.Schools Council News, No.42, Summer term, 1983.
2.It is interesting to note in this respect the very much more radical reforms being achieved at the present time in the more centralised Scottish Educational system. This includes the institution of a common system of examining at 16+ based on a wide range of novel forms of assessment and the co-ordination of post-16 school, further education and YTS qualifications. See, for example, "The Munn and Duning Reports: Research on Assessment within the Government's development programme", SED 1982 and "16-18s in Scotland: an Action Plan", SED, 1983.

* This paper was written before Sir Keith Joseph announced that a new 16+ examination would begin in 1986.

REFERENCES

Balogh,J. (1982): Profile reports for school leavers. Longman for Schools Council, York.

Broadfoot,P. (1979): Assessment, schools and society. London, Methuen.

Broadfoot,P. (1982): "Assessment and development: some theoretical and practical issues", International Journal of Educational Development, Autumn.

Broadfoot,P. (1983): "From public examinations to profile assessment: the French experience" in Broadfoot,P. (ed): Selection, certification and control: social issues in educational assessment. Falmer Press (in press).

Clark,B.R. (1982): The "cooling out" function revisited. Working Paper No.4, Comparative Higher Education Research Group, Graduate School of Education, University of California, Los Angeles.

Dore,R. (1976): The diploma disease. London, Allen and Unwin.

Elvin,L. (ed) (1981): The educational systems in the European community: a guide. Windsor, NFER-Nelson.

Ingenkamp,K. (1977): Educational assessment. NFER, Slough.

Mitter,W. (1979a): Secondary school graduation: university entrance qualification in socialist countries: a comparative study. Oxford, Pergamon.

Mitter,W. (ed) (1979b): The use of tests and interviews for selection to higher education: a European symposium. Windsor, NFER.

Orring,J. (1978): "The case for alternatives to school-leaving examinations: Sweden" in Ottobre,F.M. (ed): Criteria for awarding school-leaving certificates. The proceedings of the 1977 Conference of the International Association for Educational Assessment. Oxford, Pergamon, pp.47-56.

Ottobre,F.M. (ed) (1978): Criteria for awarding school-leaving certificates. The proceedings of the 1977 Conference of the International Association for Educational Assessment. Oxford, Pergamon.

Satterly,D. (1981): Assessment in schools. Oxford, Blackwell.

SCRE (1977): Pupils in profile. London, Hodder and Stoughton.

Shimahara,N.K. (1979): Adaptation and education in Japan. New York, Praeger.

Solberg,W. (1979): "The case for school-leaving examinations: the Netherlands" in Ottobre,F.M. (ed): op.cit., pp.37-46.

Whitty,G. (1983): "State policy and school examinations, 1976-1982" in Ahier,J. and Flude,M. (eds): Contemporary education policy. London, Croom Helm.

Chapter Two

DEMOCRATISATION IN SECONDARY AND HIGHER EDUCATION: SOME
COMPARATIVE VIEWPOINTS

W.D. Halls

DEMOCRATISATION

For the past three centuries liberty and equality have been the
two great themes of Western political discussion. Our theme in
this paper is equality, which has dominated the educational
debate since the War. If education is a vehicle for social
improvement equality of opportunity is an important goal.

Certain themes in English educational policy, such as
welfarism and accountability, are fashionable for a while - the
one originating in Crosland's views in the mid-1960s, and the
other epitomized by Callaghan's Ruskin College speech in 1975;
they then die down after having been debated, theorised about,
and half-heartedly acted upon. By contrast, the theme of
equality of educational opportunity, which has been in the
forefront of discussion for at least twenty years, refuses to
die. In one sense, it is teachers and other educationalists -
always committed idealists - who have kept this concept of the
democratisation of education alive. Parents, although their
faith in education as a panacea for all ills has now been
shattered, still cling to it as a precept of justice for their
children. Even today no British politician could afford not to
pay it lip-service as an ideal.

Nor is Britain alone in this: every Western country
professes the same goal. Like ourselves, for the past two
decades they have been busy trying to democratise their
education systems. As we look across the Channel or the
Atlantic, is there anything we can learn from them? As they
view us from the European or North American continents, can
they discern areas of our system where inequality of
opportunity sticks out like a sore thumb? The comparativist
believes that we can learn from them and that they are right in
certain respects to point a condemnatory finger at us. If, in
some points one may suspect exaggeration, it is not. Every
criticism has actually been made, on sosme occasion or another,
by a foreigner. We do not always accept the criticism - but the
fact remains that it has been made.

Moreover, we can retort that there are many points in which we are streets ahead, especially of our European neighbours. Thus our primary schools, despite some recent carping, remain the best in Western Europe. As compared with the Continent we are still far ahead in getting a larger percentage of working class youngsters into higher education. (Some 27% as compared, say, with 14% in West Germany in 1979). There is little to match the range and quality of our colleges of further education. So not all is gloom and doom. Far from it.

First, however, we must define our terms. What do we mean by democratisation or equality of opportunity? Does it mean "sameness" or "difference"? Should we treat all children alike, or give each child the opportunity to be different? The philosophers have held that the principle of equality entails treating everybody identically, except in situations where there are good reasons for treating certain individuals or groups differently. The exception, of course, begs the question. However, since about 1960, what has been termed a "liberal" interpretation of equality of opportunity has prevailed, with the result that educational policies have attempted to minimise differences in treatment of pupils or students. It is only now that the pendulum is beginning to swing, ever so slightly, the other way, with talk of children with "special educational needs" and of "education at the extremes".

The first use anywhere of the phrase "equality of opportunity" was, curiously enough, in a speech made in 1895 by Will Thorne, the founder of the Gas Workers' Union, who at the Trades Union Congress in that year moved that:

> Our educational system should be completely remodelled on such a basis as to secure the democratic principle of equality of opportunity.

That speech remained a dead letter until the passing of the Education Act of 1918, which thought that the children of the returning heroes from Flanders deserved better than they got. Likewise, in France at the same time, the movement known as the Compagnons de l'Université Nouvelle (the Comrades of the New University) was born in the French Army, the brainchild of a group of schoolteachers who found themselves serving side by side in the trenches. From that time onwards, both in England and in France, there gradually emerged the concept of the comprehensive school, which I suppose many would regard as the flagship of the concept of equality in education.

NATIONAL PLANNING AND EDUCATIONAL OPPORTUNITY

Should we indulge in more centralised planning of the economy, integrating education into it? In France the concept of indicative total planning of the economy, including social aims, is embodied in a series of national plans which, in largely four-year periods, in the past have characterised national development. Thus the Seventh Plan of Economic and Social Development, which lasted from 1976 to 1980, was expressed in terms of 25 "priority action" programmes, the totality of which was to accomplish certain aims. One of these aims was that of "reducing inequalities" and Programmes 13-17 inclusive were directed to this end. Of these Programme 13 was expressed as the task of "ensuring equality of opportunity by education and culture". (The other four programmes intended to iron out inequalities were concerned with family policy, the care of the aged, access to justice and the strengthening of the role of the consumer.) Thus Programme 13 specifically concerned education: it contained six themes, the most important of which was the equalisation of opportunity. The measures envisaged to achieve this were laid down: better education for those in the 2-4 nursery range - special attention to be paid to education in rural areas - better diagnosis of physical and mental handicaps - more aid to poorer families - the development of permanent education and adult education in general - the granting of "educational leave" from employment, especially to unskilled workers wishing to better themselves.

Programme 13 was translated into what the French called four "Actions" or "Operations".

Action 1: pre-school education. In rural and heavily urbanised areas children aged 2-3 are not well catered for educationally. The stated objective was to give some form of nursery schooling by 1980 to 45 per cent of children aged two and to over 90 per cent aged three, to reduce regional disparities and to reduce numbers in nursery and infant classes to 35 (very high by British standards). To operationalise this objective it was reckoned that 8,500 new classes were required, together with the necessary teachers.

Action 2 was concerned with ensuring that in the lower secondary school all pupils received some technical education (what Sir Keith Joseph is now advocating for British youngsters of similar age). It was reckoned that 2,000 new workshops had to be created in schools by 1980 and the necessary specialist teachers trained.

Action 3 was concerned with what is described as "cultural stimulation in the school situation", particularly of children from deprived families. In practice this meant a vast increase in the number of specialists capable of teaching drama, music, dancing, the ballet, the plastic arts and the audio-visual arts.

Action 4 was concerned with sport in school, an area in which the French have always lagged behind us. Here the aim was to give pupils a minimum of 2-3 hours per week sporting activity. For this, over the period 1976-80, 5,000 P.E. teachers were to be recruited.

National Planning (2)

This programme 13, reserved for education - but, of course, much more was spent on maintaining the educational system under the annual budget system - and envisaged a special allocation of just under 21 billion francs over the four year period. (In 1975 terms something of the order of £2.3 billion).

In the end not all the aims of the National Plan were achieved - but a great many were. What should be noted is the systematic attempt to improve equality of opportunity in various ways, first by incorporating the concept in the National Plan, the designation of a programme for it and the various "Actions" set out to achieve it, culminating in concrete steps. The only National Plan Britain has ever had, which eventually proved abortive, was that promulgated by George Brown in 1965. There may have been other attempts, but the tradition of secrecy of the Department of Education and Science, so glaring in view of the publicity accorded to French government intentions, has prevented the British public from ever knowing about them. The Organisation for Economic Co-operation and Development (OECD) review body on English education was not slow to criticise this secretive attitude or the lack of planning, when it published its now famous report in 1975. More open government, openly arrived at, would seem to be a sine qua non not only for equality of opportunity but for any sensible educational planning at all.

LOCAL AUTHORITIES: HELP OR HINDRANCE

Whether the division of England into 96 local authorities, whose duty it is to provide schools for their areas, militates against educational opportunity is a moot question. In France a centralised system operates, although for administrative purposes the country is divided into 27 education authorities, called "académies". In West Germany, each federal state (or Land), of which there are eleven in all, is autonomous as regards its school system, although there is co-ordination through a Standing Conference of the State Ministers of Education meeting in Bonn. In Sweden, although local municipalities operate the school system, all the key financial decisions are made by a Ministry of Education, although in practice it delegates most of its powers to the National Board of Education, which acts as a kind of super-LEA. In Canada each province is responsible for its schools. With the exception of the United States - although even here each federal state exercises considerable control - only Britain has so many local authorities. This decentralisation may prejudice equality of educational provision.

LEAs in England still vary considerably in size: from 110,000 pupils in the Isle of Wight to 1,430,000 in Kent - not to mention 3,000,000 in ILEA. This discrepancy in size leads to many wide variations. Thus in 1981 the London Borough of Barking spent £308.47 per head of population on education, whereas West Sussex spent only £133.69. If one compares the amount per pupil spent on books and equipment, one finds that in 1981-2 this sum varied enormously.

	Highest	Lowest
Primary School	ILEA £40.20	Leeds £6.50
Secondary School	ILEA £50.20	St. Helens £17.90

If one looks at the overall pupil/teacher ratio the range is also very wide. Leaving out the Isles of Scilly (which are nominally a county authority but in which the circumstances are wholly exceptional), we find that in ILEA the overall ratio stood at 14:2, as contrasted with the Metropolitan District of Oldham, where it was as high as 20:8. Moreover, we know that pupil/teacher ratio does not reflect the even larger number of pupils that a teacher is usually teaching; nevertheless, a difference of even 6 pupils a class is considerable. On another yardstick - the percentage of 3 and 4 year olds in nursery and infant classes in 1981 - vast differences exist between the regions, not to mention the LEAs. The North has 64 per cent of toddlers in nursery education, the South-West only 22 per cent.
Enough figures have been cited to demonstrate that our system provides varying equality of opportunity according to where you live. In other countries they order it differently. In France the "School Map" divides up the territory into "school districts", on a kind of grid system, which stipulates within each district what should be the variety and location of educational institutions, depending upon population size. Furthermore, all teacher appointments are made nationally, as are all promotions and repostings. (This system is not as iniquitous as it sounds: commissions composed equally of Ministry representatives and the teachers' unions decide upon the allocation of teachers. Teachers posted from one area to another receive resettlement allowances and, if they move to a more expensive area, are entitled to receive additional salary allowances.) National norms are laid down for size of classes. If a head teacher finds that the norm is exceeded, then he or she has the right to ask for an additional teacher and a parallel class is formed. Usually repostings are made with the consent of or at the demand of a teacher. The teacher languishing in the smoky industrial North can ask for a more congenial post on the French Riviera. If he wishes to pursue his studies part-time, he can ask for a transfer to a

university town. The really ambitious pedagogue, from the academic viewpoint, may want to be in Paris. Indeed it is often said that the success of a French teacher is in inverse proportion to the kilometric distance from Notre Dame of his post. The point is that disparities, whether in spending, in pupil/teacher ratio or in any other way, can be ironed out centrally, thus giving children a more equal chance. Incidentally, the French are often shocked at the "teachers' market" advertised weekly in the <u>Times Educational Supplement</u>, and the fact that teachers may be appointed by local people who are not professionals. They claim that this is bound to lead to abuses.

What does seem apparent is that 96 local educational authorities such as exist in England provide a patchwork quilt of provision rather than a uniform spread, which would seem desirable.

STRUCTURES

Since Circular 10/65 the English school system has acquired no fewer than twenty-two different points of entry and exit to it. In secondary education alone six different patterns are found, ranging from the "all-through" comprehensive, the "middle school" or institutions with a break at 13, 14 or 16. This surely cannot make for equality of opportunity. A youngster who moves from one part of the country to another at age 13 may find himself translated from a secondary school back to a middle school "deemed primary", with all the differences this entails in curricula, methods and ethos.

As Diagram I demonstrates, this is much less liable to happen elsewhere. In the United States the most common pattern is 6 + 3 + 3 (although 6 + 6 systems and 8 + 4 systems do still exist). In West Germany, where the tripartite secondary system remains the usual form, a comparatively small number of comprehensive schools has been started experimentally. Bavaria has a handful, while Berlin and Hessen are almost totally comprehensive. Elsewhere, however, the patterns are stable. Incidentally, the diagram shows up two other features. Whereas in England the 11+18 secondary school system survives as the most usual form, in other countries the pattern is for a new start to be made in a different kind of school at about the age of 16. The idea of a new beginning for later adolescence has much psychologically to commend it and chimes well with equal opportunity. All start again with a clean sheet. The other feature in the diagram is that other countries start school later than in England although in France there are pressures to lower the primary school starting age.

The chart is misleading, however, because all the other nations shown here have a flourishing nursery system. In England, ever since the Plowden Report of 1967, the pundits have told us that schooling of some kind for the under-5s is an

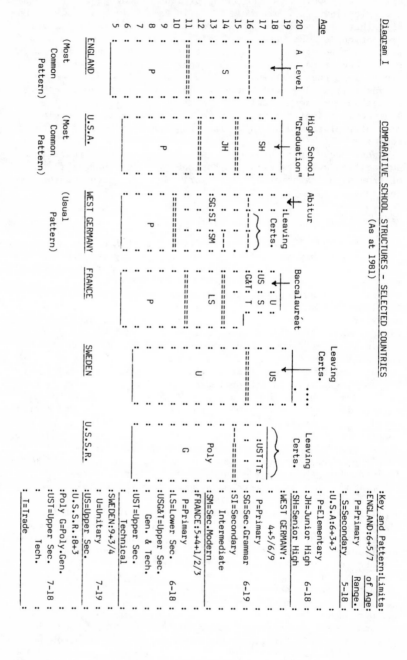

Diagram I

COMPARATIVE SCHOOL STRUCTURES – SELECTED COUNTRIES
(As at 1981)

ideal way of reducing inequality. Whereas in Greater London 49 per cent of 3 and 4 year-olds were in nursery schools in 1981, in other areas the proportion was far less: in the Trafford district of Greater Manchester, 16 per cent; in West Sussex, Avon, Dorset and Kent, 13 per cent or under. Contrast this with France or Belgium or the Netherlands, where 80 per cent of 3 and 4 year olds are already in nursery schools. In France, by the age of 5, all children are, as in England, also in school. In this area we have enormous ground to make up.

LOWER SECONDARY CURRICULUM

In England today the debate about a "common" or "core" curriculum for compulsory secondary education rages unabated. It is one that is the more acrimonious because teachers fear that their professionalism is threatened, maintaining that laymen are not qualified to decide what should be taught. Yet in a situation where each secondary school has, within extremely wide limits, the right to decide the content of the education it dispenses, inequalities are bound to arise, particularly at the crucial age of 13-14 when options begin to operate. In one school a child may be given the opportunity to do physics; in another he may only be offered photography. Some schools have separate courses in history and geography; others offer only social studies. Some schools offer three separate sciences, others integrated or general scientific studies. The catalogue of variations is endless, particularly when we come to the more exotically named courses, such as "Design for Living". It is hard to see how this diversity of choice between schools promotes equality of opportunity.

Other countries have produced a standardised curriculum, to which all lower secondary schools must adhere. Three examples are given here: Italy, France and Sweden. (See Diagrams II, III and IV). Two features are noticeable: first, the number of "hours" (or lessons per week) is prescribed; second, for all children the curriculum has been, as the subject titles imply, one with an academic bias. This is confirmed when one looks at the detail of each particular discipline or group of disciplines, which is also usually prescribed - although the degree of prescription may vary. In France, for example, syllabuses are laid out in considerable detail, and even methods are largely prescribed; in Sweden only aims and objectives and general guidelines as to content are set down. English teachers may throw up their hands in horror at such standardisation and exhaustive detail. In reality, things are not as bad as they sound. In the elaboration of curricula in Sweden it is the National Board of Education, on which serve many teachers, which is responsible. Even in the most centralised country, France, joint commissions of inspectors and teachers are responsible for what is taught. Thus a child who moves from one part of the country to another will find the same curriculum operating and roughly the same content in each subject. Surely this offers greater equality of opportunity than the haphazard approach that prevails in different schools and authorities in England?

Diagram II

LOWER SECONDARY CURRICULUM

Italy - Scuola Media (11-14) (1979)

	Year 1	Year 2	Year 3
R.I.	1	1	1
Italian	7	7	6
Hist., Civics, Geog.	4	4	5
ML	3	3	3
Maths. and Sciences	6	6	6
Tech. Ed.	3	3	3
Artistic Ed.	2	2	2
Musical Ed.	2	2	2
P.E.	2	2	2
	30	30	30

Democratisation in Secondary and Higher Education

Diagram III

LOWER SECONDARY CURRICULUM

France (1980)

	Years 1 & 2	Years 3 & 4*
French	5 + 1 hr extra help	5
Maths	3 + 1	4
ML	3 + 1	3
Hist. - Geog.	3	3
Exptl. Sc.	3	3
Artistic Ed.	2	2
Tech. & Handicraft Ed.	2	1 1/2
TOTAL	21 + 3	21 1/2
P.E.	3	3
Optional Sport	2	-

In years 3 and 4 pupils take ONE of:

Latin 3 hrs - 2nd ML 3 hrs - Technology 3 hrs - Greek 3 hrs - 1st Language enrichment 2 hrs.

School year = 35 weeks.

Length of "hour" = 50-55 mins.

* 4th year pupils, where necessary, are given extra remedial classes.

Diagram IV

CORE CURRICULUM

Sweden - Grades 7-9 (Age 14 - 16) (1979)

Swedish	10
Maths	12
English	9
R.I., Hist. and Civics	16
Sciences	15
Music	2
Art	5
Craft	4
Home Economics	4
P.E.	9
Child Care	1

TOTAL CORE	88
+ Electives* up to...	17

MAXIMUM	105

* e.g. Fr./Ge./Aesthetic
        Practical/Soc. Studies/Sc. (Bio.)
        Technical
        Group work in "care" subjects.

As we saw, when examining school structures, many countries have now moved on to what we would call a "sixth form college". Today in Britain there are still only some 120 sixth form colleges, although between them there is great diversity. In the more affluent areas of the country - in Solihull, Stockport, Hereford and Nuneaton for example - where colleges have developed out of old, well-established grammar schools, access is restricted and all students attending the colleges are studying for A Level subjects. By contrast, West Park College, Sandwell, has some 45 per cent on non-A level courses. The average over the whole country of non-A level sixth formers in Colleges is 21 per cent, about the same as in sixth form in schools. Unless such colleges are open-access institutions all that has happened is that the 11+ selection has been moved up to a 16+ selection. There are surely cogent reasons for youngsters of 16-19, of whatever academic ability, to be educated together, so as to ensure a mixing of the various social classes at a critical age.

UPPER SECONDARY CURRICULUM

In the United States the model of the senior high school - grades ten through twelve - shows three tracks existing side by side: academic, vocational and general. But the Swedish example probably corresponds even more to the ideal of equality of opportunity. There are 23 different "lines", between which the youngsters can opt at age 16, with courses of two, three or even four years in length. The two-year courses provide for a wide variety of occupations, each based upon research into the labour market and job possibilities; the three-year courses - four in all - lead on to higher education; the one four-year course leads to a junior engineering qualification. If these connote three levels, the vertical division is into three types of course: arts and social subjects (7 lines); economics and commercial subjects (3 lines); technical and scientific subjects (13 lines). Just 90 per cent of all Swedish young people continue their education in these courses beyond 16 (as compared with about 40 per cent in school and F.E. Colleges in England - a figure that should give cause for concern, since, as compared with other Western countries, England, as in nursery education, is lagging far behind).

What is more, the never-ending saga of what should be the education for those aiming at higher education, with all its arguments and counter-arguments regarding specialisation, is not one that is understood elsewhere in Europe, where specialisation in the English sense is unknown. This means that final decisions regarding future career or courses in higher education need not be taken until the end of secondary education.

EXAMINATIONS

Regarding examinations, the quarrel about the A level examination in England and Wales has dragged on for over twenty years without being resolved. It is now apparent that there is a similar argument about an examination at 16. Should it be a common system of examining or a common examination for all children? This argument is also liable to continue for years even though it has been decided that O level and CSE should cease to exist as from 1986. Meanwhile, England is the only country in Western Europe that has any kind of examination, in the sense of a formal written test, with essay-type papers, at the age of 16. Everywhere else the formal evaluation has been abolished. (See Chapter One for a further discussion of this point). For the variety of qualifications that the young Frenchman can acquire at ages 16 and 17 the rule is one of continuous assessment and entrance to the equivalent of the sixth form in Sweden is not entirely dependent upon success in a previous examination. This seems inherently fairer than the English procedure, where at 16 the youngster is subjected to CSE/O Level papers in which, despite efforts to camouflage failure, only two thirds are likely to succeed. The disappointment and failure engender discouragement and reinforce a feeling that schools lead to inequality.

The A level quarrel, which has never been finally resolved, ended with proposing a solution that was remarkably like one that had been put forward at the beginning, twenty years earlier. Yet this "sudden death" examination, in which one in three is bound to be rejected, has been retained. Abroad more reasonable systems have been adopted, in which continuous assessment of work done in the last two or three years of schooling may either be the sole criterion or an important element in an evaluation, which may also be accompanied by standardised tests. This does not apply to France, which holds its baccalauréate in as much reverence as a "sacred cow" as the English do their A Level. In the United States, however, the cumulative credit-unit system is used without harming standards. Moreover, high school graduation is achieved by the overwhelming majority of students, although not necessarily in what Europeans would consider to be the more important subjects. Of course, the American student who aspires to enter one of the most prestigious colleges or universities still has to have credits in subjects such as English and Mathematics. The flexibility of the system is, however, that graduation is virtually assured for everybody in some combination or another of subjects. In Sweden success in a final leaving examination is secured on school record and performance in a series of objective tests in the main subjects, administered at intervals during the last two years of the course. In West Germany a record of class work is kept and assessed with the results of a written conventional examination in the main subjects that have

been studied, together with the possibility of an oral
examination in those deemed less important. All such measures
seem intrinsically fairer than the A level system.

GROUPING

Let us turn now to pedagogical practice. There is considerable
division in the West as to whether homogenous or mixed ability
teaching is the better way of promoting equality of
opportunity. After considerable research (such as the Stockholm
study) Sweden´s unitary school for 7-16 abandoned all streaming
devices: all pupils, save in two or three options which only
operate in the top grade, are taught together in all subjects.
This, it appears, does not inhibit the very bright from forging
ahead and enhances the progress of the less bright. This seems
admirable until we learn that up to 40 per cent of children are
taken out from their classes - not, of course, the same
children each time - in various subjects - to receive special
help. This procedure would appear to be "remedial" treatment in
all but name. The Swedes are not particularly doctrinaire as
regards mixed ability classes but regard them as the lesser
evil. Ideally, they say, each pupil should have his own tutor:
in other words, equality of opportunity is best ensured when
instruction is individualised, but they realise that this is an
impossible ideal.

By and large the Americans also insist upon mixed ability
teaching, but this is tempered in two ways. Firstly, in Grades
10-12 three tracks are available - the academic, the vocational
and the general. Secondly, the level at which a pupil studies a
subject can be varied: for example, a Grade 12 pupil - in his
or her last year of High School, therefore - may be taking
Grade 10 English only, namely, for English, he or she studies
with Grade 10 pupils for that subject, whereas in Mathematics
he or she may be doing College level work.

The Russians, like the Swedes, are in favour of mixed
ability teaching, partly on ideological grounds: they subscribe
to the view that it is not genetic ability but environmental
factors that are the determinants of school performance. The
theory is that if children are falling behind it is because of
their home environment rather than because of a lack of
brainpower. However, like the Americans, at the age of 16 they
separate into three tracks: the one reserved for the more
academically inclined, anaother for future technicians, often
of a high grade (school teachers at primary level are included
in this category) and trade schools for manual workers.

The French, following a European trend, have, like the
English, at least maintained mixed ability teaching for the
first two years of lower secondary education. This innovation
dates from 1977 and has not been well received by everybody,
particularly the teachers, who agitate for the scheme to be
abandoned. The quarrel, as usual, follows party lines among the

politicans. The Right argue that it is unfair to the less able pupil never to be given the chance to shine because he is always outdone by his brighter fellows in the same class. The Left argue that what is called "le brassage social" - "social mixing of classes" - is as important as the intellectual advantages and disadvantages. Certainly one of the purposes of a common secondary school, as it at present operates in many, if not most, European countries, is to promote equality by means of mixing all children up together as much as possible. Arguments are advanced that this will prevent, in later employment, the development of negative attitudes, a "we and they" mentality arising between employers and employees. Such arguments are cogent but, as in this country, modern language teachers and mathematics teachers everywhere appear to view the new system unfavourably.

PRIVATE EDUCATION

Can a truly democratic education for all be provided if private, non-state schools are allowed to exist? Sweden argues that it is not possible, and has accordingly banned all private education except for four special schools for diplomats and others. In France, however, the Catholics still educate some 15 per cent of the school population. The present Socialist Minister of Education, Alain Savary, has re-opened old wounds and provoked demonstrations by wanting all non-State schools to become part of the State system. There have also been a few other private schools, some Protestant, such as the Ecole Alsacienne, others secular, such as the Ecole des Roches, which have been modelled on the English public school. In West Germany private schools are attended by about 4 per cent of the school population, although the private Gymnasium, the grammar school, which is the road to university, accounts for about 10 per cent of all those attending this type of school. As in France, many such private schools are denominational, this time Protestant as well as Catholic. Apart from religiously-orientated schools, other private schools in West Germany are those based upon a particular kind of educational philosophy. Thus, in the Landersiehungsheime, schools located in the country, outdoor pursuits are as important as intellectual ones - the kind of "outward bound" activities exemplified in the school at Salem founded by Kurt Hahn who, upon the coming to power of the Nazis, came to Britain and founded Gordonstoun and, much later, Atlantic College. There are also a few schools based upon a particular Weltanschauung or world philosophy, such as the Rudolf Steiner schools. Both in France and West Germany, however, it must be admitted that the private system is thriving, because of what is alleged to be the indiscipline and low standards in State schools.

It would be ludicrous, however, to compare such schools as the Jesuit college where de Gaulle's father was director of studies, to institutions such as Winchester and King's College, Canterbury, which date back to the Middle Ages. Attendance at a private school on the Continent confers no particular distinction and initiates you into no exclusive "old boy network", as it is alleged to do in England. Nor, in the prestigious universities of France and West Germany do we find, as we do in Oxbridge, over 40 per cent of the students originating from non-State schools. The argument for the abolition of private schools in France is not because of privilege and social class, but much more because of the age-old quarrel, as the French poet Aragon put it in another context, of "He who believed in Heaven, and he who did not". In other words, the argument is religious. Nevertheless, we should perhaps ask ourselves whether it is not time that our famous public schools were turned into sixth form State boarding colleges, open to an intellectual elite.

ELITISM

If you were, however, to argue that the existence of an elite is incompatible with democratisation, the practice of such diverse countries as France, the United States and the Soviet Union would contradict you. Provided that entrance to elite institutions is restricted to the best, regardless of social class, these countries affirm that there is nothing that militates against equal opportunity about them.

In France the crucial institution is the "grande école", at university level, but much more prestigious than the university faculty. Presidents of France, radical, socialist or neo-Gaullist, have passed through such institutions as the Ecole Polytechnique (started, curiously enough, to prepare military engineers for the Revolutionary armies) or the Ecole Normale Superieure (started to provide grammar school teachers), which lead on today to the most influential posts in society. Entry to such institutions is through an intensely competitive examination, taken after two years in certain prestigious Parisian or provincial "lycées" - State sixth form colleges - at post-A Level. Even to get into these two-year preparatory courses, which, although still given in school, are really at university level, is extremely difficult. In America, where some form of higher education is open to practically everybody regardless of ability, even although it may only be in some obscure State college, the equivalent is entrance to an undergraduate course at an Ivy League university - Harvard, Yale and the rest. In the Soviet Union outstanding talent - perhaps 0.1 per cent of the age group - is picked out earlier, between 10 and 14, for entrance to specialised institutions such as language schools, scientific schools or artistic schools (for ballet, for example), usually boarding institutions, entrance to which is by a national competition each year known as Olympiads.

Even a democracy cannot neglect to cultivate its best brains if it is to survive in the modern world. Today the public schools/Oxbridge route to the top is called into question but there is no doubt that some such unique institutions should be accepted for our education system. In any reform throwing out the baby with the bathwater must be avoided. Instead the opportunity to compete should be open to all and not simply the favoured few.

GOVERNANCE OF EDUCATIONAL INSTITUTIONS

The theme of "participation" of the application of democracy in the running of universities and schools, has become topical since the Taylor Report of 1977. This topicality is apparent elsewhere.

In West Germany the professoriate - which did not include even the lecturers - had run German universities on a somewhat authoritarian basis. In 1968 this began to change. Student unrest provoked the principle of co-management. Professors, other academic staff, non-academic staff and students were all represented, equally in some cases, on faculty committees, university councils, etc. Students, acting in concert with the other partners, could outvote the professors on academic matters, even those relating to teaching and research. However, after certain cases had been taken to the German Federal Constitutional Court it was ruled that this procedure was unconstitutional. The judges said that the professor, in his department, had responsibility for his subject, including the research undertaken. If the German example seems extreme, it must be seen in the context of the early 1970s as much as the student revolts of 1968: the former was a period when what were termed "co-determination models" were being set up in German industry. Some of these have functioned very successfully in German economic life and have enabled West Germany to avoid some of the confrontations between employers and workers which have characterised the English industrial scene.

In France, what was termed "co-gestion" (co-management) and "participation" were written into the Faure Law of 1968, which attempted to bind up the wounds of the May Revolt. Students were also called upon to take part in the running of their universities. The experiment has not been altogether successful and moves have been made to hand back some of the powers granted to the professoriate. It was found that in elections for student representatives on various university bodies, only 10-20 per cent of students bothered to vote at all. The candidates were politically strongly to the Left. They attended meetings when matters of financial advantage to students were being discussed, but were slack about matters of normal university business, which of course are those that occupy most of any committee's time. Maurice Niveau, one time the top educational civil servant, has written somewhat acidly about this politicisation of higher education in the name of democratisation. He quotes the famous French actor, Jean-Louis Barrault, who draws a distinction between "contradiction" and "contestation" in his comments upon the student occupation of the Odeon Theatre in Paris in May 1968:

> We are at the moment passing from the age of contradiction to the age of contestation. Contradiction implies the recognition of the opposing party that one seeks to contradict. Contestation systematically refuses to acknowledge any opposing party, suppressing a priori the existence of the antagonist. The person contesting contests the very existence of him who is contesting.

There would seem to be a lesson for us somewhere in this - and not only in the educational field. The fact remains that students today have a voice in the running of every university in Britain. Whilst none would wish for the clock to be turned back, it does seem questionable as to how far those who enjoy a privilege for which the rest of us are paying should be able to overrule the judgement of those whom we pay to run our universities and teach our students. Which is the more democratic viewpoint?

What of democracy in the schools? The following quotation from Der Spiegel of 27 March 1972 in an article entitled "In almost every class, unrest and conflict" illustrates the problem well. The quotation reads:

> When the asthmatic physics teacher enters the physics lab on the fourth floor, he is gasping for air: (He says to the class): May I open the window for a moment? Answer: First we must vote on it. Nobody is in favour. "The window stays shut".

"Pupil participation" was introduced in West Germany for two reasons: firstly, as a result of the unrest of 1968, which spread to the schools; seconly, and perhaps more important, as an attempt to make German democracy, still a tender plant hardly more than a generation old, real to pupils. Thus in Hamburg a school law was proposed instituting what was to be known as the School Congress - in effect, a kind of Parliament, which would be elected in three equal sections by parents, pupils and teachers - with any two (say, parents and pupils) capable of outvoting the third. The school "parliament" would be able to decide on the distribution of the school's budget, school rules, including timetable and breaks, the authorisation of school political groups and the use of school buildings after school. Pupils would be able to vote in each form from the age of 14 onwards. Moreover, - and this was a real novelty, - the assembly would also appoint a headteacher, who would be subjected to a two-year trial period and remain in office for only ten years. In another German federal state, Hessen, ever since 1970 pupils aged 16 and over have been entitled to vote upon matters concerning the school rules, criteria for marking and for promotions, the nature and extent of homework and the application of the authority's rules and regulations. Furthermore, the head teacher is disenfranchised. Numerous other similar plans were put forward in West Germany in the early 1970s. Interestingly, the teachers' unions took opposing positions about pupil participation: the GEW, the main teachers' union, thought that it had not gone far enough; the Philogenverband, the grammar school teachers' union, took the opposite view.

Since the later 1970s, however, the atmosphere has changed. Elected School Councils are the rule in West Germany, but nowadays parents and pupils can usually be outvoted by teachers.

In France also the "conseil d'administration" or governing body comprises representatives of all sections of the school community, including pupils. Pupils have access to other bodies, such as the conferences of teachers where the vocational and educational guidance to be given to pupils is discussed, including the progress of a particular class. However, once individual cases are debated, pupil representatives must withdraw. Pupil strikes, which were the bane of the 1970s, are today comparatively rare. When they occurred, they were highly politicised and any attempt, for example, to intervene in a "sit-in" of the school premises was likely to draw support for the pupils from some extremist party or even from the teachers' unions.

In Sweden, where the social and political climate is more moderate and less extreme, in civics courses, as part of the inculcation of democratic values, pupils are shown exactly how peaceful demonstrations should be conducted. Thus, for example, one class investigated the pollution by factories of a local stream, analysed the chemicals, traced the commercial undertakings involved, prepared a case for presentation to the local mayor and the press and carried out Saturday morning demonstrations, with placards and slogans, all with the full approbation of the school.

Thus democratisation, participation, co-management and what might be described as political education are all entangled together. The 1981 Education Act, in England and Wales, based as it was upon the Taylor Report, has attempted to involve the local community, including pupils, more in the running of its schools. How much farther we should go along the road is a matter for debate. Goverment Proposals are now for parents to have a majority vote on school governing bodies. School Councils, in some form or another, exist in possibly half the English secondary schools, replacing the allegedly outmoded perfect system. Should we also, as some advocate, introduce full-blooded political education, with the teaching of political and social skills such as bargaining, compromise, etc., as part of the curriculum? Such a proposal inevitably arouses strong political partisanship but it is not as unrealistic as many people think.

CONCLUSIONS

It would be wrong to draw hasty lessons from a very selective number of topics relating to secondary and higher education. The emphasis has been on ways that other countries tackle problems of equality of opportunity, in an attempt to highlight ways in which we in England and Wales still seem to be deficient. This does not mean that we can adopt their solutions. What is appropriate in one cultural context can be very inappropriate in another, as is shown by the experience of Third World countries which have had solutions to their problems thrust upon them from the industrialised countries. But as we think afresh attempts to achieve greater equality of opportunity perhaps the comparative dimension may be one element in our thinking and may help towards the realisation of that ideal.

Chapter Three

POST-COMPULSORY EDUCATION, 16-19: COMPARISONS AND CONTRASTS
ABROAD TODAY, AND AHEAD FOR EVERYONE

Edmund King

A CHANGED CONTEXT

Ten years ago, in 1973, two colleagues and I completed the 5-
nation survey of "Education 16-20", which we had been
conducting for 3 years and which we reported in the two volumes
Post-Compulsory Education I: A new analysis in Western Europe
(King et al, 1974) and Post-Compulsory Education II: The way
ahead (King et al, 1975). About the same time, the Council of
Europe had been mounting a number of meetings between senior
officials and inspectors of education, supported by the
collection of printed evidence from member countries. These
resulted in the publication of a policy report by Henri Janne
and Lucien Geminard on The Educational Needs of the 16-19 Age
Group (Strasbourg, 1973) and a large body of country-by-country
information in a separate volume under the same title. There
were also a number of parallel investigations of "Education 16-
19" in individual countries or special areas within them,
because the "16-19s" were suddenly in the news at the end of
the expansive and optimistic 1960s.
    In the ten years since then the context has changed
momentously. Politicians justifying the mess they made and the
ommissions for which they are culpably like to refer to the
"crises" of fuel and finance which became insistent after 1973
(multiplying the cost of energy fivefold, accelerating
inflation, and aggravating, but not causing, unemployment). Of
course, these factors have had a profound influence on all
social and political decisions, especially those affecting the
youngest adults; but in essence those decisions about
"education and careers" or "education for the future" or indeed
about the content and style of education for the "16s to 19s"
could long have been foreseen as inevitable. The fact that
crises have arisen in education since 1973 (especially in post-
compulsory education) has been the result of social and
political conservatism compounded by scholastic unwillingness
to reconsider the content and phasing of education to meet
headlong and accelerating technological change.

The prospect of continuous and penetrating change in education itself (as an inevitable consequence of change around the schools and ahead of them) is reflected, for example, in titles like Compulsory schooling in a changing world (OECD, 1983), but it is on the young adult frontier, when compulsory schooling has ended, that prospects are most clearly uncertain and that existing provision is most obviously inadequate for tasks whose nature constantly changes. Phrases like Education for Uncertainty (King, 1979), which seemed paradoxical in the early 1970s, are built into the deliberations of educators today - especially in all that concerns the transition from compulsory schooling to adult life of whatever type.

This conceptual change is of central importance to educational discussion of young adults' present circumstances and future prospects. Indeed, the phrase "young adults" was still unused for students in secondary schools or training (or even for their contemporaries outside) when my colleagues and I began to use it in our report. Most educational and political discussion referred to "young people" or "youth" or - in Britain especially - "children". As late as 1983 we still hear of "Youth Opportunity Programmes" and the like, referring to young men and women, who in important respects are legally adults and who are much more so socially.

Hence those who think about education for the over-16s or even the over-14s increasingly have to recognise that participation and partnership in their own education are essential. Indeed, the management and planning of education for the young adult age-group have been enlightened already by "participant research" of the kind that my team initiated; it has been followed up by Ministerial consultations, by much wider and more active acceptance of students' contributions to planning and programming and by the enlargement of "self-directed" studies (with joint consultation, of course). How different all this is from what is implied in the Italian title "Ministry of Public Instruction" or by the battery of separate channels of education-or-training provided (often by distinct Ministries) after the end of compulsory schooling - all with a view to separated career styles, perennial categories of competence and different life-futures based upon tight packages of learning!

In the perspective of lifelong uncertainty about unemployment, about job-changes, about the whole occupational structure and its international relationships, the youngest adults have become a political problem of the utmost importance - even in their own right, partly because they now have the vote at 18 in most developed countries. Moreover, the key position of today's young adult frontier, where people aged 16 to 25 constitute about half of all the growing number of unemployed and where the average duration of any job is 6 months, has already begun to be significant for an increasing number of middle-aged, middle-class persons with good professional preparation, whose jobs or marriages suddenly fade away. Even if jobs become available, fresh preparation and personal reorientation are demanded. Thus the craving and the need for "a fresh start" which so characterised young adults' responses to our investigations a decade ago are now central to all thinking about "post-compulsory education". We have to see "post-compulsory education" as provision for an educational level, through which many pass at the end of compulsory schooling, but to which many adults (young and old) return after intervals of varying length and experience.

That is the major educational change in the context of discussion since the early 1970s, but there have also been changes in the nature and extent of communications of every kind since then. Microprocessors, the computerisation of information services, worldwide and immediate access to the exchange of ideas and experience - these things are a familiar part of every young adult's life at home, increasingly so at work and indeed often at school. A few school and college systems positively reorganise their programmes to avail themselves of the logical consequences of these innovations - "discontinuous" programmes of study-and-work in and out of one course or establishment, the use of "alternative educators", different programming of the school day, flexible grouping of students, "permeable membranes" between institutions and levels and so forth. Far more of this kind of thing must inevitably come at all post-compulsory stages, but not least at what might be called the immediately post-compulsory level of the youngest adults. Through that level ("from 16 to 19 or 20") an increasing percentage has been passing; to it a rapidly increasing percentage returns because of unemployment; and to it (in some form, and by different means) a majority of today's younger workers will have to return because of occupational changes introduced technologically or for international reasons.

It is, therefore, in a context drastically changed since the early 1970s that we must consider what has been and what is still our neighbours' way of providing "Education, 16 to 19".

"THEY DO IT DIFFERENTLY" - WHO DOES, AND TO WHOM?

In most countries of the world it is assumed that a Ministry or Department of Education provides and regulates a clearly demarcated system of formal education throughout the country, province or large-city area for which it is responsible. Indeed, most of these administrative systems are national. Teachers are public employees in the sense that civil servants are in Britain. Programmes, examinations, promotion systems and mechanisms for transition from one level to another are officially regulated from the centre. Usually a small minority of schools are independent and most of these are generally of lower esteem and inferior academic standing.

However, when that generalised picture is drawn we at once recognise that exceptions especially occur in post-compulsory education. Ministries of Labour or Agriculture or Commerce, etc., may run particular schools or colleges. Major industrial and commercial enterprises, independently, of the state may provide training courses leading to certificates recognised by the state, even though the state claims a monopoly of "general" examinations. Within the period of compulsory schooling itself there may be distinctly administered programmes entitled to special subventions (like vocational education in France). In Britain we had never known anything of the kind until the interventions of the Manpower Services Commission in very recent years.

One consequence in many continental countries of Europe has been that especially at post-compulsory level school/college/training systems have been and are precisely docketed - each type of establishment with its designated kind and level of intake of students ("pupils") for specific "package-deal" courses whose constituent elements cannot be changed because they follow defined curricula leading to specific, official examinations and are taught by teachers in a hierarchy of civil-service status according to defined qualifications and closely circumscribed commitments in the curriculum. On the other hand, there may be much hidden variation within the schools or courses. Students may be of surprisingly different ages. The programming may be arranged in a way that permits students (as well as teachers) to come and go; and both students and teachers may be part-time, working somewhere else during the rest of the time. Intermittent attendance by students, private conversations at the back of the class, beards in the classroom and smoking in the corridors are of little concern to the teachers, who may seldom meet each other to discuss progress of individuals or groups. Indeed, teachers may tell you that they are "really a chemist" or something other than a permanent teacher. those who are permanent teachers may serve part-time in a university or college elsewhere, or a teacher-training establishment or in some other public service.

Indeed, the British tradition that teachers and pupils are in school and belong to it is seldom observed in a large part of post-compulsory education elsewhere. Consequently, even in these days, most over-16s in Britain seem by contrast to be surprisingly docile, dependent and juvenile. On the other hand, the generally co-operative self-disciplined informality of British sixth-form colleges and tertiary colleges would seem like a dream in many continental establishments. Though the high politicisation of the 1960s in continental post-compulsory schooling has faded, nevertheless a very considerable hiatus remains between the schools´ expectations and the students´ social or personal aspirations. Few are committed to the sort of society and career structure implied by schools´

organisation and curricula; students comply, pass the examinations if they can, but generally "do their own thing". In the large number of countries where schools are organised on an incomplete-day basis (i.e. until about 2 p.m.), many students are in paid employment part- or full-time (if they can find it, as they often can in the "grey economy" of untaxed enterprises). Thus continental students in Europe and many more in the less industrialised parts of the world are already men and women of experience beyond the ken of British over-16s. Thus direct comparisons of organisation and discipline are very hard to make.

Many countries' school systems, too, have the secondary stage marked into two distinct cycles, which nowadays seldom coincide with the legal age-frontier between compulsory and post-compulsory education. Even in the lower-secondary school, it should be remembered, "repeating" classes means that many pupils are over-age by several years, perhaps, for the classes they attend. The teachers in the upper-secondary cycle (themselves often subdivided into categories as described above) are often considered superior to those teaching in the lower-secondary cycle and elementary schools. They may share the title of higher education teachers (e.g. "professeur") as well as some of their functions. In fact it is common to recruit university teachers from among the specialists of upper-secondary schools. For all these reasons, and others, there is often felt to be a real break between the lower-secondary cycle and everything that follows. The upper-secondary cycle of traditional academic schooling may have a different name from the first cycle (e.g. lycée, liceo, Gymnasium) and be in a separate building dating from the time of an earlier educational organisation, when perhaps (as in Scandinavia) elementary and lower-secondary education were a local responsibility whereas upper-secondary education in the gymnasie was a state affair. For this reason too teachers may be paid and moved around by distinctly different methods even now.

Thus all forms of post-compulsory education are frequently seen as a stage beyond (and different in kind from) whatever occurs in the compulsory age-range. At the risk of over-simplifying it is rather like the transition from "secondary" to "tertiary" education in Britain - rather than the mere continuation into a "sixth form" in an "all-through" British school. That is so even in the more academic classes comparable with but more exacting than British grammar school traditions; and the transition from compulsory school to something "post-school" is more noticeable in the Germanic and Southern-European forms of organisation whereby a large proportion of the education offered after the age of 14 or 16 (according to the country) is provided in "technical" or "vocational" institutions (istituti tecnici or professionali, Fachschulen, etc.). Certificates gained in such establishments usually confer precise legal rights in connection with specific trades, but until very recently they have not been usable for admission to further or higher education. Hence formal hierarchies of course and qualification have become ossified, reinforced by tight examination arrangements.

The great loosening-up began from about 1961 onwards, being contemporary with, but not necessarily influenced directly by, the development of comprehensive secondary schools. The extension of that comprehensiveness into the post-16 phase in Sweden opened up the way to a more flexible future - educationally and in terms of careers - because it gradually brought together within one system of post-compulsory education both the need to continue general education and the opportunity to specialise around that "core" according to present attainment and subject choice.

POST-COMPULSORY EDUCATION: GRIDIRON OR OPEN-PLAN?

The kinds of self-contained and rigidly compartmentalised types of post-compulsory schooling described above as separating "general" programmes from a multiplicity of distinct vocational courses still continue, and are likely to exist for a long time in some countries; but in all the most industrially developed countries ⋆ and especially those recently hit most severely by unemployment and the electronics revolution - a very important tendency has gathered pace during the past decade. Let us take stock of this change, both structurally and operationally.

We are all familiar with the diagrams contained in UNESCO and similar handbooks setting out the bare bones of educational comparisons. We are shown that in nearly all countries now elementary (primary) education takes place in a single track. (Private schooling in the British sense is rare at that level, and indeed independent secondary education is usually an insignificant factor in other systems´ educational and social life - an important point often overlooked!). From that single-track elementary provision the early stages of secondary education to the age of about 14, 15, or 16 have gradually become more similar, or have been blended or made "equivalent", or have been combined in a "single middle school" as in Italy in 1963 and Leicestershire later, or indeed have been incorporated in an extended basic school (grundskolan in Sweden and its counterparts in Norway and Denmark). In effect, the whole of compulsory schooling is therefore supposed to take place in a unified or closely blended system of comprehensive education, though we must never forget that local peculiarities (such as "repeating" or shortage of buildings and suitable teachers) may prolong hidden segregation for decades.

Therefore, most official "snapshots" of school systems in the early 1980s show a solid trunk of basic education to the age of about 11 or 12, continuing upwards and perhaps broadening out until the age of about 14, 15, or 16, and then

- only after the end of compulsory schooling - diversifying a little in choice of subject but not now into huge or widely separated branches. Instead, indeed, of snapshots we in the 1980s have come to expect live "video" presentation: in place of the firm gridiron structure still found almost everywhere before the 1970s we see the steady evolution of an adaptive provision. I do not mean only that the provision is adaptable - though that is true - but that the intention is increasing by adaptive: to help people to share more in their present and future education, on the flexible basis of opportunities made available in post-compulsory education.

Whereas the earliest moves towards comprehensive schooling during the compulsory stage rightly laid emphasis on much closer sharing of common premises and a common heritage of curriculum (perhaps diversified round the edges to suit individual aptitudes, needs and paces), post-compulsory education´s recent moves in the same direction have generally provided for two apparently distinct elements at the same time: (a) a strong body of "shared" curriculum and educative experiences together; (b) distinct opportunities for individual or group aptitudes, needs and paces around that shared curriculum - presented as far as possible in ways showing both the complementariness of distinct interests and their necessarily incomplete nature. On this account, the need to be ready for change and later adaptation is often emphasised and, on that account again, "self-directed" studies and the use of alternative learning contacts are brought into prominence. Of course, computer-assisted delivery of some kinds of instruction (especially technical, but also bibliographical and otherwise "arts"-linked) links learning with resources and experience beyond the institution´s walls in ways now familiar to all young adults.

In addition, the intervention of outside agencies (such as the Manpower Services Commission in Britain and Ministries abroad which are comparable in function) exercises a most powerful influence - far beyond the expectations and traditions of previous Ministry of Education norms. Despite the rigidities and separations still enforced by whole batteries of examinations and certificates, present tendencies increasingly take account of the national need for education and training as a whole - increasingly, too, in an international perspective. In fact, some traditional rigidities are broken down by governments´ official recognition of technical and pre-professional qualifications awarded by large employers and entrepreneurs, even in countries where such alternatives would not be countenanced for "general secondary" education.

In Britain as well as in the great big world outside which we have so often tried to ignore in education, alternative structures and interactions in higher education of course make rigidities at the upper-secondary level more than ever obsolete. If higher education is available on a vast scale in alternatives to the traditional universities (for example, in new technological universities, in polytechnics, institutes of higher education or in Open Universities) - sometimes available to people without formal admission requirements or with "odd" combinations of credentials and experience - that situation makes nonsense of the "gridiron" course structure and hierarchies of pre-university institutions of the past. Furthermore, the alternation between work and study, work and training, between qualification and post-experience re-qualification, indicates increasingly that many or most previous procedures for selection-for-a-lifetime are now in question for academic and professional reasons as well as for reason of social policy. The revolution in education thinking that this consideration implies can best be seen simply by looking back on all those "gridiron" upper-secondary and technical structures in the provision for post-compulsory education between about 1945 and 1973 and by remembering at the same time that precisely foreseeable proportions of the population were envisaged then as being permanently channelled into each type of structure. From the 1980s onwards we must always think of adaptable provision for unknown quantities of people and their yet unforeseeable needs in the technological and social uncertainties ahead. The dawning recognition of this truth is slowly enlightening the world's realisation that post-compulsory education for the rest of this century will be very different from what we painstakingly learned about during the 1960s and 1970s.

POST-COMPULSORY EDUCATION: FOR WHOM?

Even at the time of our research into post-compulsory education referred to above, (King et al, 1974, 1975) staying on at school to the age of secondary school completion had become much more nearly universal in some countries than in Britain. In the early 1970s the Japanese percentage of full-time enrolments had reached 85% of the age group (it is now 95%); in Sweden it was about 85%, in the United States over 80%, in Norway 75% and in many other countries the proportion enrolled far exceeded the shameful British 30% - almost the lowest in Western Europe. Furthermore, the rate of increase in such enrolments was even more remarkable than the total, since it represented a doubling or trebling in about two decades (i.e. well before the crises of post-1973). The fashion of pre-1973 was to consider that newly enrolled population by the measure of those previously enrolled: many spoke of "assimilating" the "newcomers" as though they were migrants (and indeed in some sense they were geographical as well as social migrants); others spoke of adjusting school programmes to the present aptitudes of those whose previous education had been inadequate, on the assumption that they might "catch up" to join the rat-race of qualifications, etc.; still others thought of adjusting courses to the needs of girls and rural newcomers. But hardly anyone recognised that the whole scholastic apparatus for post-compulsory education (perhaps also compulsory education) was now in question, and that the real challenge was to envisage post-compulsory provision as the first stage of adult education - the first step in a lifelong process of continuous education and re-education for everyone, in a perspective of perennial change.

Such a declaration may seem like a pious platitude, but on the contrary it has become a practical problem of catering not so much for "youth" or for "16 to 19s" as for whoever wants or needs to learn at that level. The first steps taken in post-1973 to provide for "youth" not in school or work were clearly an attempt to correct a dangerous social situation - "to put out the fire of youth unemployment", and the same endeavour continues to be a major element in contemporary "youth" training or re-training schemes throughout the industrialised world. Indeed, many of the emergency schemes developed do not lead to permanent employment or even to any employment at all. In any case, because of rapid technological/occupational changes referred to earlier and the whole preponderance of young adults in the unemployment and short-term employment statistics, the entire relationship between the "16 to 19" level and the transition to a working life is at present undergoing intense scrutiny both by providers and by young adults themselves. (OECD, 1983). Often the insights derived from those who come fresh or who return to education at this level (Anderson and Blakers, 1983) are more pertinent to education in the long term than the "gut reaction" of those recognising only a problem of "youth" or "transition to work", and in any case, the learners' own changing experience and consequential recognition of altered educational needs (Borghi, 1983) must be reckoned in any evaluation.

By that last remark I take account of significant changes in those learning at the level previously thought of only in terms of "Education 16 to 19". So great has been the influx of new enrolments at about that level that the Manpower Services Commission in Britain has already become the nation's biggest employer - mainly concerned with vocational/technical training in the wide "post-compulsory" range between the standards of education and competence expected of normal 16-year-olds and the normal intake-level for higher technological education. (A note for students of Comparative Education: you do not keep out "centralising" governmental control merely by not having a "centralising" Ministry of Education, which in other countries than Britain would probably have kept such interventions more closely under educational control.) Because of Britain's peculiar circumstances, the newcomers in education and/or training at post-16 levels mostly come from that more than 60% of the age-group who have never previously been enrolled at that age. In other countries they might well have been voluntarily enrolled there already; and then the adjustment of their education and training to suit present and future needs would have been more easily and more nationally responsive to long-term prospects.

Britain tends to think of young adults' education and training as an "emergency" response, whereas for a long time now a process has grown abroad of recognising that all workers have a right to "Paid Educational Leave" which will enable them to improve their education and vocational qualifications - usually consisting of about half a day a week. Most European countries have now legally established that right. Elsewhere, or in addition to PEL, the practice of "coming back" to education as and when wanted or needed has become a regular feature of young adult life, as, for example, in Sweden since the 1960s and in France since the 1970s. This practice is facilitated by some governments' willingness to recognise an educational "entitlement" to the equivalent of full secondary completion for all, though this entitlement can be taken up in stages or after an interval. Sweden guarantees education or training as an alternative to employment, if that cannot be found, until the age of 25. Sweden, Italy and several other countries, including the Soviet Union, admit "late-comers" to higher education without formal qualifications above the age of 25. All these innovations have profound implications for any consideration of "Education 16 to 19" in future. No less important in the long run, however, is the recognition of the plural constituency served by post-compulsory education for the rest of this century. (King, 1980).

To take but one example - the breakdown of so many marriages has precipitated a return to education and training, often at quite early "post-compulsory" levels, of many women. Not many women in employment can afford to take them off during the day, but some can do so part-time and others return to colleges of further education where they join younger adults "topping up" or reorienting their previous education at levels previously associated with upper-secondary school or modest further education. All these adults learn together at that level with no problems because the style is different and the content, though often essentially the same, is differently slanted. Other adults attend such provision to "top up" science or languages or to learn additional elements of these things in association with previously acquired competences. Differences of background or professional status are of little or no account. How different from previous "post-16" education and the "sixth-form" circumstances in which it is/was carried out!

Britain can be more venturesome in these respects than most other countries, mainly for two reasons: (a) our long tradition of adult education in huge variety and in the multiple circumstances of local education authority and "voluntary" provision; and (b) our tremendous need to catch up hurriedly with the educational and training achievements of very successful neighbours around the world. Britain, therefore, has much experimentation to offer as an example - but only if reciprocally Britain recognises its dire need to make vastly more and better provision available for those previously "short-changed" in education. The most fertile ground is in post-compulsory education: there the need is most urgent, most recognised and most likely to be responsive to world tendencies and needs, if we invite the young adults of all the world to contribute the insights of their experience and aspirations - as we tried to do in our researches a decade ago.

NOTES AND REFERENCES

Anderson,D.S. and Blakers,C. (1983): Youth, Transition and Social Research, Australian National University Press, Canberra, discuss in international terms both "transition from school to work" and the views and experiences of "returners".

Borghi, Lamberto (1983): "Youth perspectives on the Future", Comparative Education, Vol.19, No.3. Shows how attitudes of young adults enrolled in "16 to 19" institutions have changed remarkably between the 1960s and 1980s.

King,E.J., Moor,C.H. and Mundy,J.A.: Post-Compulsory Education I - A new analysis in Western Europe (1974), and Post-Compulsory Education II - The way ahead (1975). Both published by Sage Publications, London and Beverly Hills.

King,E.J. (1979): Education for Uncertainty, Sage Publications, London.

King,E.J. (1980): "Education's steps towards computer-assisted learning", European Journal of Education, Vol.15, No.2, discusses the general implications for education of the need to re-learn (often by electronic means, and in mid-career).

See the OECD Observer, passim, and OECD: Education and Work - The views of the young, (1983).

Chapter Four

SEX BIAS IN EDUCATION, AT HOME AND ABROAD

Margaret Sutherland

INTRODUCTION

Sex bias in education is international. In any country of the
world we can find some differentiation of schooling and higher
education according to the sex of the learner. But it is also
noteworthy that in the last two decades there have been
attempts in most, if not all, countries and continents to
reduce this bias and, especially, to improve the access of
females to education. The results vary from country to country
and the amount of differentiation varies. Perhaps initially we
should remind ourselves that if we think equal opportunities in
education are important we must bear in mind that, whatever the
defects which sex bias may produce in education in the British
Isles, we have at least in this country, as in other
"developed" countries, (as UNESCO describes them) greater
access of both males and females to education than in many
other countries of the world. Some UNESCO figures(1) illustrate
this point clearly. In 1979 the percentage of age groups of
children and young people in full-time education was as
follows:

Age Groups	Developed Countries		Developing Countries	
	Males	Females	Males	Females
6 - 11	93.1	93.3	75.4	60.5
12 - 17	81.9	84.3	44.9	32.6
18 - 23	33.6	30.8	14.2	8.1

We see that females may even be slightly better represented
than males at secondary education level in developed countries
as a whole, but disadvantaged, as compared with males, at
higher education level. In developing countries, both sexes are
disadvantaged as compared with their counterparts in developed
countries, but the greater disadvantage of females is obvious

and striking. If we feel disposed to lament the slowness of progress towards equal opportunity for both sexes in education in developed countries we can at least note than in these more affluent countries of the world females suffer much less disadvantage in education than in the others.

Consequently, in making comparisons it is usually with other developed educational systems that we are concerned. As the figures have indicated, progress seems to have been made to virtual equality of access at secondary education in developed countries. Equality of access does not necessarily mean equality of opportunity: other factors such as the types of institution entered and the courses followed may greatly increase or reduce opportunities. But let us begin by considering the level at which, in some developed countries, including our own, there remains clear inequality, that is, the level of higher education. It is here that more must be done if satisfactory provision for female education is to be made.

HIGHER EDUCATION: WOMEN IN UNIVERSITIES

International statistics on "higher education" may be confusing in referring to a variety of institutions. If we focus on universities, rather than "third level" institutions in general, we find that there has been great improvement in women's access to this form of education during the last two decades. In the UK in 1962, the percentage of women students in universities was 27; in 1981-82 women were 40.7% of those entering university.(2) (Scotland was slightly better than England, with 43.9% compared to England's 39.7% of women among entrants; Wales had 43.3%). But the British progress has been surpassed by that made in other developed countries. In the United States, in Canada and in Poland, women are 50% of the university student population. In the US indeed there has been noticed a slight tendency now for women to outnumber men where entries to higher education in general are concerned. In such countries as Finland and East Germany there is in some years a slight majority of women, from 51% to 54% among those entering university. The UK admittedly is not at the foot of the league table of developed countries in this respect: some European countries still have a lower percentage of women students at university than we do - Switzerland, for example, managed a mere 32% in 1979 and the Netherlands 30%. France, however, just about reached equality with 49% in 1979.(3)

But two points have to be kept in mind in making such comparisons. As we have noted, statistics may refer to a great variety of institutions within a country - in the United States, for example, women may outnumber men in the less prestigious universities and be outnumbered in the more prestigious. Similarly, in Japan, women may be more often found in two-year "universities". In France, one has to take into account the competitive entry of the Grandes Ecoles, those highly respected institutions with excellent vocational prospects for their graduates: here, apart from the Ecoles Normales Superieures, which are closely related to upper secondary teaching careers, women are usually heavily outnumbered, by about 8 to 1.(4) So simply looking at university statistics does not give the exact picture of women's position in higher education.

The second point is the position of teacher education. School teaching at primary and pre-school levels is considered a woman's profession in all countries. At secondary level too it is increasingly being "feminised" in many countries. Now where teacher education is undertaken by universities - and there is a commendable trend for this to be increasingly the case - the numbers of women going to university to train as teachers may give a misleading impression of the whole situation of women in universities. The variety of courses taken by women and the range of careers open to them may be much less than those for male university students if in fact the majority of women are concentrated in teacher education.

Yet even making these allowances, it does seem as if women have achieved greater access to university education in some other developed countries than in the United Kingdom. We have to ask ourselves why this should be so and whether our situation could be improved.

Inequalities are even more evident and requiring thoughtful consideration at the second and third levels of higher education, the levels at which masterships and doctorates or equivalent qualifications are taken. Here, alas, we find that even in the highly developed educational systems and the most progressive countries there is a reversion to the situation in which women are clearly in a minority. Even though great determination was shown in past struggles to get women students into universities, there seems to have been a relaxation of effort and even some degree of apathy, where higher degrees for women are concerned. A typical situation was noted by the Carnegie Commission on Opportunities for Women in Higher Education in the United States.(5) Reporting in 1973, the Commission highlighted the remarkable lack of change in the proportions of women taking mastership or doctorate degrees between 1920 and 1970. The actual numbers of women had increased, of course, with the increase in numbers of students in higher education, but the proportion of those achieving doctorates remained remarkably similar throughout the period; masterships showed some improvements towards the end of the period but still did not reach equality with the proportion gained by men. But in the United States there have been signs of progress since then. In 1979-80 the percentage of women receiving masters' degrees was 49.4; at doctorate level, it had reached the promising but still satisfactory percentage of 29.5.(6) (These figures may be compared to the 1964-65 levels, when the percentage at Master's level was 33.8 and, at

Doctorate level, 10.8). While one must still make some allowance for the dominance of Education as a field of study for women postgraduates in the USA, it would seem that there has been marked improvement in the situation in the United States. Certainly the figures cited seem more encouraging than those for European countries at these levels. In the German Democratic Republic, for instance, the percentage of women among those achieving Promotion A (the first postgraduate qualification) in 1979 was 27.1 and Promotion B (which is probably rather higher than the British or American Ph.D.) 9.3%.(7) It is difficult to find exact figures for masterships and doctorates in the UK: normally official statistics merely give percentages of males and females among postgraduate students and this can be misleading, because many women postgratuates are taking a one-year teaching qualification (the PGCE). But among those obtaining higher degrees in the UK in 1981 women are about 27% of the total:(8) subdivisions for masterships and doctorates are not given in the Universities Statistical Record.

Thus at the highest levels of education the United Kingdom seems, like most, if not all, developed countries, to have failed to encourage women. It may, of course, be that women themselves are not interested in going on to take such qualifications: the reasons for such lack of interest could be varied, including the reason that in many countries, besides this country, there is little expectation in society generally that women will go on to higher degrees. They may not be encouraged by their university teachers to proceed further. Women themselves may not see themselves as likely to enter the careers for which higher degrees would prepare them, for example, the career of university teacher. In that career certainly women are still under-represented. Britain is approximately equal to West Germany in having between 2 and 3 per cent women among university professors; France and Finland are better with some 6 per cent; the DDR has an estimated percentage of 10-12. Schools in this country announce with pride the success of former pupils in achieving university entrance and first degrees. Perhaps they should now emphasise higher degrees as objectives for both boys and girls. Certainly the evidence indicates that in some countries more progress is being made by women at the higher levels of higher education. In East Germany indeed universities have committees whose function it is to study the position of women on the staff and to encourage more women to achieve higher qualifications and make progress in careers as university teachers. It would be good to find similar trends and encouragement in the United Kingdom.

SUBJECT CHOICES

But it is not simply a matter of achieving access to higher

education and to higher degrees. It is important to consider what subjects are studied in higher education as, indeed, it is important to consider what subjects are studied in school. Choice of subject determines the kind of work which is open to the individual: the choice of subjects at school may determine the range of occupations which can be successfully opted for later.

There is very general international agreement as to the kinds of subjects which are boys′ subjects and girls′ subjects just as there is much agreement as to the occupations which are for men and those which are for women - though countries may sometimes differ here. Obviously there are few absolute divisions in these respects, but there are very clear trends in certain directions.

If we take the UK situation first, we find the following percentages of female students at undergraduate level in different subject areas:(9)

Biology	54.7
Medicine, dentistry, pharmacy	42.1
Biochemistry	41.1
Agric., forestry, vet. science	36.4
Maths	27.9
Chemistry	23.9
Physics	13.4
Engineering	6.7

These figures may be contrasted with the majority situation of women in the languages and the Arts.

The situation in medicine is particularly interesting since, until recently, there was in British universities a kind of quota system for admission of women students in Medicine; only recently has this been abolished and places awarded on qualifications without regard to gender. Hence there has been a considerable increase in female entrants so that, whereas in 1962 only 22% of medical students were women, they are now at about the 40% level. This is a particularly interesting example of a subject in which a social or academic policy seems to have counteracted natural inclinations of individuals. Many girls are attracted by the idea of medical studies: some of the earliest battles to get women into universities in different countries were waged on behalf of those wishing to become doctors, and in other countries, notably the USSR, the percentage of women among doctors is very high (though this is at first qualification level only). So too in associated medical studies, women in other countries tend to be in a majority. In Finland the majority of dentists are women. In France and other countries, women dominate in Pharmacy. (In France women even constitute 45% of the university teaching staff in Pharmacy, though mainly at the lower levels of appointment.)(10) There are some signs that in Britain also women are tending to be in a majority in this subject.

Britain has been out of line with some other countries in its earlier limitations - though prejudice against women in medical faculties has not been unknown in other countries. But in other subjects, notably the applied sciences, the trend in Britain is the same as that elsewhere: enrolment of females is low. In Maths and Natural Sciences too females have been in the minority in Britain and in other countries. The preceding table demonstrates a typical position, e.g. despite recent efforts to recruit girls for engineering only 6.7% of students there were female.

The situation could, it would appear, be changed. If we look at figures for university students in the German Democratic Republic(11) we find this situation:

	Percentage of women students
Medicine	57.1
Maths. Natural Sciences	45.4
Technical Sciences	27.0
Agricultural Science	47.9
Economics	57.5
Social Sciences/Art	39.4
Education	74.1
Literature/Languages	70.9

Certainly there is reinforcement of the view that women seek out or are mainly found in literature and language studies and much less found in technical sciences. But it is interesting to note the actual percentages of women found in Maths, Natural Sciences, Agricultural Science (which admittedly includes food processing) and even Technical Sciences. While women may be in a minority they are well represented in Maths and Natural Sciences. Even in technical sciences they are much more strongly represented than in the UK universities. It looks as if, to some extent at least, the sex bias in subject choice has been reduced.

We find confirmation of the reduction of bias in the occupational sphere when we look at the percentage of girls in vocational training or apprenticeships for various occupations in East Germany:(12)

	Percentage of females in training
Chemical industry	50.6
Electronics	46.1
Machine construction	32.1
Mechanics	43.4
Data processing	81.7

But this, of course, ties up with the situation in the labour market of different countries. The supply of qualified workers and the demands of the country's economy must affect willingness to maintain or eliminate barriers to one sex or the other in certain occupations.

SCHOOL SYSTEMS: OPTIONS

We are thus led to look at the school systems which have produced or supported sex differences in subject choices. What strikes us as a distinguishing feature of the systems in the UK, France and some Western European or American countries, compared with schooling in the German Democratic Republic (and the Soviet Union and other countries of the Soviet bloc) is the availability of options for pupils in secondary education. In the British systems, pupils in secondary schools can drop certain subjects which they dislike or which they feel are of no particular value to them (or, just possibly, which the school timetable will not allow them to take in conjunction with other subjects they decidedly want to take). This system of options in secondary school means that in examinations at the end of that period there are very clear indications as to which are girls' subjects and which are boys' subjects - or are thought to be so. Figures from the DES Statistics of Education repeatedly demonstrate the superior percentages of girls in French, Biology, Music and Cookery, while boys are found to be dominant in percentages in Maths, Physics, Technical Drawing and Woodwork.(13) This is a situation familiar in other countries also. Options for the school leaving/university entrance baccalauréat qualifications in France showed these percentages in 1979-80:(14)

	Percentage of female candidates
Latin - Modern Languages	82.6
Maths. - Biolog. Science	55.1
Maths. - Physical Sciences	37.1
Agric. - Tech. Sciences	28.2
Technical Sciences	4.3

In the technician's baccalauréat which has options related to various branches of industry, there was an 11.1% entry from girls; options associated with medical and social studies had a 98.7% female entry.

Now in the DDR - as in the Soviet Union - the amount of options pupils can undertake during full-time schooling is strictly limited, less than 10% of the timetable. In the basic ten-year comprehensive school the distribution of time is this: maths/natural sciences - 29.8%; social studies/mother tongue/literary-artistic studies - 41.1%; introduction to socialist production and productive work - 10.6%; foreign language - 10.6%; sport - 7.9%.(15) In the top classes only two or three periods a week, out of 34-35 periods, are given to optional studies. (Of course, pupils can develop their special interests further by attendance at leisure-time classes and study circles). Similarly, in classes 11 and 12, for those who continue in full-time secondary schooling, 75% of the timetable is given to the common curriculum, which includes maths., physics, chemistry, biology, history, geography, civics and sport as well as German, Russian and a second modern language.

In conditions like these, girls do not have a chance to opt out of maths and sciences as they all too frequently tend to do when options are offered. Girls also have to engage in the same practical productive work with machines as the boys do. Hence they must enter the labour market later with at least a basic grounding in skills which, in other systems, would be regarded as sex-differentiated. Boys must study foreign languages as well as sciences.

One must indeed recognise the possible importance of a compulsory common curriculum with regard to the learning of foreign languages as well as maths and science. In our own schools, there is, as we have noted, the tendency to think of foreign languages as more the preserve of girls. It might therefore be a very good thing if boys' avoidance of this subject could be reduced - though one recognises that compulsion is not necessarily the ideal method. In fact, there has been in recent times a tendency for the study of foreign languages to become generally less important in our schools. The position of "minority languages" is especially threatened as relatively few pupils study them and fewer teachers become available: there is less demand for the languages, so posts for teachers of these languages become harder to obtain, so fewer people are encouraged to train as teachers of such languages. The contraction of schools as pupil numbers become smaller is likely to accelerate this trend: the "luxury" of a teacher of languages studied by only a small proportion of pupils is something that schools will not be able to afford. In this way, more and more pupils are likely to leave school without any real foreign language competency and the variety of languages studied will be reduced. It is true that English is a world language and that English-speakers have the advantage in that so much is written in the language and so many people in other countries are willing to learn English and use it. (Foreign politicians seem to do very well, speaking English in media interviews.) So ours would seem a poor education system which sends out people who have not benefited by this kind of study. From time to time governmental pronouncements do stress the need for scientists and engineers to know other languages: more generally, such pronouncements include this study as an essential component of a good education. Membership of the European Community also seems a reason in favour of improved language skills. And yet the study of foreign languages has diminished in popularity and boys more than girls seem likely to suffer from lack of learning here. It has to be admitted that in France and Western Germany also there have been signs that pupils are not enthusiastic about foreign language learning and in particular the reform of the West German Abitur (equivalent of A-levels) has meant that pupils have more freedom of choice of subject and thus may study English less than before. But it seems to be in the British systems that the amount of freedom of choice given to pupils has most damaging effects on language learning.

Of course, there are problems in making all pupils study a common core curriculum to an advanced level. Some concession has to be made in the amount of time given to individual subjects: fewer periods may mean - though not inevitably - lower levels of achievement. It may be necessary also to study some subjects in alternate years rather than uninterruptedly. Specialist interests could be developed by extra-curricular work. These changes might be worth making to avoid the dangers of too early decisions to drop subjects: the introduction of sex bias in choice of subjects could at least be postponed.

For one must recognise that a common curriculum for most of school education does not necessarily eliminate sex bias in subject choice. In Sweden various forms of comprehensive school were tried out experimentally during the 1950s, with varying degrees of choices open to pupils.(16) Eventually the system evolved to one with very little differentiation of the timetable (only some five periods per week) until the end of the nine-year basic comprehensive school at age 16. But in the upper secondary school pupils may opt to follow a variety of "lines" and in pupils' choices of lines the familiar sex differentiation is widely evident: males opt for technically biased courses, girls for textiles, languages, arts and social sciences.(17) Yet at least in such cases both boys and girls have achieved a basic competence in the full range of subjects, before embarking on options.

We may note in passing another curious effect that options have occasionally had on the school careers of boys and girls. In the Swedish experiments, when the choice of a foreign language option was required for admission to the upper secondary school, girls tended to qualify more often than boys in this way: there seemed at one point a danger that the upper secondary would be "swamped" by girls though, as we have noted, this particular option system was not long-lived. In Finland, more recently, it has been possible for pupils at the junior secondary level to opt for different levels of difficulty in courses in certain main subjects. Girls more often than boys have opted for the higher (intensive) levels in such courses and have consequently tended to outnumber boys in the higher secondary classes for which such courses formed an entrance requirement, though here also the system has now been modified. In passing also one may note that there is some international evidence that girls achieve rather better than boys in secondary school. In France, at baccalauréat level,(18) in Finland at upper school-leaving level(19) and in class 10 of the basic East Germany 10-year school,(20) girls have been tending to get rather higher marks or pass more frequently than boys. In England, also, girls tend to have a better pass record at O-level though not - as yet - at the three A-level stage.(21)

CO-EDUCATION

One of the aspects of school systems which might affect sex bias is the type of school, co-educational or single-sex. Clearly when schools in the past were set up to provide secondary education specifically for girls they emphasised for their pupils the study of domestic subjects and aimed to provide studies thought particularly appropriate for the female sex. But such specialised schools for girls have been dying out. Indeed there has, during recent decades, been a world-wide movement (except in Muslim countries) towards co-educational schools.(22) In many countries it has been confidently expected that co-education will eliminate sex bias in education since both sexes have the same teachers, timetables and facilities. In practice, it has not worked out like that and this is particularly evident if we look at countries such as the United States, which have had co-educational schools for a long time. In many countries which now have co-education we find that sex differences in subject choices, especially at higher education levels, persist. It has been found, in this country and in others, that if girls are to be encouraged to specialise in mathematics and science, girls' schools may be more successful in fostering such choices, since in such schools there may be fewer influences to suggest that these subjects are not for girls. It depends, of course, on the attitude of teachers and the attention that they give to individual pupils. But it seems rather unfortunate that there has been such enthusiasm in many countries for co-educational schools since comparisons of the effects of single-sex and co-educational schools are going to be difficult to make in future, few single-sex schools surviving or those that do survive being uncharacteristic of the general population in other ways - e.g. by selection as to social class or religion. On the other hand, it may be noted that more than one country has affirmed that co-education is particularly good for boys.

REAL SEX DIFFERENCES?

It could be argued that consideration of the situation in other countries leads to the conclusion, not that they provide better for girls than we do, but that the results of education in other systems confirm a theory that there are innate preferences and abilities in males and females for certain subjects and activities. Since many educational systems reveal the same sex bias in choice of subjects, it could be said that they are simply conforming to biologically determined differences. It is true that the International Evaluation of Achievement series of investigations carried out in different subject areas, each assessing performance in the subject in a number of countries, did seem to confirm some of the expected differences in performance between the sexes. Girls, for example, showed some superiorities in reading comprehension(23) and literature(24) while boys did better in maths.(25) and physical sciences.(26) But there were considerable differences in the level of performance of boys and girls in different countries. The performance of Hungarian and Japanese girls in chemistry, for example, was better than that of boys in other countries - though not as good as the respective performances of Hungarian and Japanese boys. In physics, the Japanese girls' score was equal to that of the average score for boys in the countries included in the investigation.(27) So it would seem that gender does not set an absolute limit on achievement but that the teaching in a country - and possibly also the country's attitudes towards achievement - can decide how effectively girls and boys will learn any subject. The achievement of the Hungarian and Japanese girls indicates that girls in other countries should be able to reach at least those levels. Similarly, as one of the researchers on the learning of French as a foreign language points out,(28) boys may do less well in learning a foreign language in countries where such learning is regarded as somewhat effeminate. Boys in countries where foreign language learning is regarded as important and indeed essential are likely to perform rather better than boys in countries where it is seen as less "masculine" a study. Thus, while common sex biases appear in a number of countries, we also find that achievement is not necessarily limited by gender and can be much affected by social attitudes. (Since reference has been made to the International Evaluation of Achievement Studies, we can remark that they did not quite answer a question which they might have been expected to answer - which country produces the highest level of achievement in various subjects? Which country, in fact, has the "best" educational system? The reports of the international studies[1] had to contend with too many complicating variables - for example, the choice of test items to suit pupils in different systems, problems of translation, sampling of pupils from different types of schools, length of time for which pupils study certain subjects in different countries, total length of compulsory schooling, early or late "loss" of pupils from the school system. So the question cannot be answered, perhaps fortunately. Some countries tend to do well overall; some do well at one age level, less well at others; some do better in one aspect of a subject than in other aspects. From a national point of view, one has the impression that neither England nor Scotland tended to come out at the top of the league tables in the subject studies in which they participated: with variations according to subject and age level of pupils, a happy "middle" position seemed most likely in comparisons).

ATTITUDES TO SEX ROLES

So far we have noted that there are some similarities and some differences in the position of male and female students when we compare what our educational systems offer with what is offered in other countries. But, especially since it has been suggested that certain attitudes are widely found and affect strongly the kind of education and employment offered to males and females, there is also the question of what different educational systems are doing - or not doing - to modify existing attitudes towards the role of women and men in work and in society generally. In some instances this question is being tackled directly as part of the school curriculum. Sweden, for example, has included in its civics lessons for a long time now discussion about sex roles in society and the rights of women.(29) This topic in civic education seems to have enjoyed moderate popularity among both pupils and teachers. Yet it is difficult to judge how far such teaching has been effective in modifying attitudes. Probably Sweden has made much progress in giving equal rights in society and in fostering acceptance of the view that the two sexes should share equally in tasks associated with running the house and looking after children. (In the Scandinavian countries there has been introduced provision for paternity leave as well as maternity leave). Yet as we have noted, there is still considerable sex differentiation in choice of subjects. Finland, in a Government statement of a policy for promoting equal rights and opportunities, has proposed to develop teaching about equality as part of subject teaching,(30) but as yet it is too early to judge whether such teaching will prove effective in modifying attitudes. While various countries are trying both approaches - direct discussion of attitudes and roles, introduction of carefully chosen materials as part of the study of other subjects - it is not yet clear what effect such approaches can have in modifying society's attitudes. It is difficult for schools to put across new views of sex roles if the experience of everyday life counteracts these views.

Similarly questions arise with regard to girls' and boys' learning about citizenship and politics. Some countries include civics - with discussion of human rights - as part of the basic school curriculum for everyone. In Britain, after many years of women's suffrage, we have a remarkably small number of women MPs, even if one woman's contribution to the political life of the country has been extremely notable during recent years. Studies of political knowledge tend to show that boys are better informed than girls in this respect - and not only in this country.(31) We might again compare our situation with that of Finland where the proportion of women in Parliament is 25%. Would the participation of females in local and national government be increased if our school system, like that of other countries, included systematic teaching of civics? Would sex differences in this respect be reduced, even if some still remained?

CENTRALISATION

But here we meet with a point that is highly important in making international comparisons. It is that most, if not all, countries in Europe with whom we might compare ourselves have a centralised curriculum. They know not only what subjects all their pupils will be learning but pretty well what will be learned within these subjects. The oddity of our educational systems is that we cannot say for certain exactly what choice of subjects pupils at various points in secondary education will have and what they will be taught within these subjects. External examination syllabuses admittedly may offer some useful guidance (though CSE Mode III illustrates diversity) but such syllabuses don't tell the whole story. So, when we ask whether they do it better abroad, we should also ask "better than whom?" or "better than which of our schools?" It is in some ways easier to know what other systems do than what we ourselves are doing. Individual schools and individual teachers in our systems may be doing admirable work in civics teaching, in studying sex roles, in working to encourage subject choice on individual grounds rather than on sex stereotyping. But this good work co-exists with work in other schools which do not care about such matters and are content to reinforce the old attitudes and the old prejudices - consciously or unconsciously. Hence, there might be something to be said for more centralisation of our system, for more agreement as to what is done in certain vital respects: some common policy with regard to girls' progress in maths and sciences, boys' progress in foreign language learning, might be advantageous, some general agreement about studies relevant for all citizens of the country. How such common policies are to be arrived at is debatable: possibly better communication, consensus rather than central dictation, would be the route to follow. But we do have to consider whether the very flexibility of our educational systems allows stereotypes to persist where more resolute centralised policies in other systems may at least be getting rid of some of them and developing all pupils' talents more effectively.

NOTES AND REFERENCES

1. UNESCO (1982): Statistical Yearbook.

2. Department of Education and Science (1967): Statistics of Education, 1965 and U.G.C. (1983): University Statistics, 1981-82, (Cheltenham, Universities' Statistical Record), Table 7, p.25.

3. UNESCO (1982): op.cit.

4. Ministere de l'Education (1981): "Annee 1979-80: Effectifs Post-Baccalaureat", (Vanves, Service et Etudes Informatiques et Statistiques).

5. Carnegie Commission on Higher Education (1973): Opportunities for Women in Higher Education, (New York, McGraw-Hill Book Company).

6. Perun, Pamela J. (ed) (1982): The Undergraduate Woman: Issues in Educational Equity, (Lexington Books), p.54.

7. Ministerium fur Hoch-und Fachschulwesen (1980): Hochschulen und Fachschulen der DDR: Statistischer Uberblick, (Berlin), p.33.

8. U.G.C. (1983): University Statistics, (Cheltenham, Universities' Statistical Record), p.8.

9. Ibid., Table 9, pp.28-29.

10. Ministere de l'Education (1979): "Note d'Information", (Vanves, Service des Etudes Informatiques et Statistiques).

11. Ministerium fur Hoch-und Fachschulwesen (1980): Hochschulen und Fachschulen der DDR: Statistischer Uberblick, (Berlin), p.25.

12. Staatliche Zentralverwaltung fur Statistik (1975): Die Frau in der DDR, (Dresden, Verlag Zeit im Bild), pp.38-39.

13. Deparment of Education and Science (1982): Statistics of Education, (London, HMSO), Vol.2.

14. Ministere de l'Education (1981): "Note d'Information", (Vanves, Service des Etudes Informatiques et Statistiques).

15. Gunther, K-H., et.al. (1979): Das Bildungswesen der Deutschen Demokratischen Republik, (Berlin, Volkseigener Verlag), p.55.

16. Royal Board of Education in Sweden (1958): Survey of the School System in Sweden, (Norrkoping, Aktiebolaget Trycksaker), p.43, and Boucher, L. (1982): Tradition and Change in Swedish Education, (pergamon), pp.88-90.

17. Sutherland, M.B. (1981): Sex Bias in Education, (Oxford, Blackwell), p.54.

18.Ministere de l´Education (1981): "Note d´Information", (Vanves, Service des Etudes Informatiques et Statistiques).

19.Central Statistical Office of Finland (1980): Position of Women, (Helsinki), p.26.

20.Staatliche Zentralverwaltung fur Statistik (1975): Die Frau in der DDR, (Dresden, Verlag Zeit im Bild), p.36.

21.Department of Education and Science (1982): Statistics of Education, (London, HMSO), Vol.2, pp.32-33, 54-55.

22.De Grandpre, Marcel (1970): La Coeducation dans les Ecoles Officielles et les Ecoles Catholiques de 45 Pays, (Montreal, Universite de Montreal).

23.Thorndike,R.L. (1973): Reading Comprehension Education in 15 Countries, (John Wiley & Sons).

24.Purves,A.C. (1973): Literature Education in 10 Countries, (Almqvist & Wiksell, John Wiley & Sons).

25.Husen,T. (ed) (1967): International Study of Achievement in Mathematics: A Comparison of 12 Countries, (Stockholm, Almqvist & Wiksell).

26.Comber,L.C. and Keeves,J.P. (1973): Science Education in 19 Countries, (Almqvist & Wiksell, John Wiley & Sons).

27.Kelly, Alison (1978): Girls and Science, (Stockholm, Almqvist & Wiksell).

28.Carroll,J.B. (1975): The Teaching of French as a Foreign Language in 8 Countries, (Almqvist & Wiksell, John Wiley & Sons).

29.Marlund,S. (1977): Civic Education in Swedish Schools since 1945, (Stockholm, National Board of Education).

30.Council of State, Finland, (1980): National Programme of Finland for Promoting Equality between Women and Men, (Helsinki).

31.Torney,J.V. et.al. (1975): Civic Education in 10 Countries, (Almqvist & Wiksell, John Wiley & Sons).

Chapter Five

EDUCATIONAL POLICY AND PROVISION FOR A MULTI-CULTURAL SOCIETY

Keith Watson

INTRODUCTION

In the early 1960s, the idea that Britain might become multiracial, multilingual or multicultural (with the exception of the Scots, the Welsh and the Northern Irish) was almost laughable. One undertook teacher training courses in Teaching English as a Foreign/Second Language to work abroad or to work amongst student visitors or _au pair_ girls in the various language schools in London or along the South Coast. By the middle of that decade, however, (that is by the time I had returned from teaching in Pakistan to help establish a department specialising with immigrant children in a secondary modern school in Leeds in 1966) it was obvious that something dramatic and challenging was happening to British society. There was a sense of crisis, of urgency. The sudden influx of large numbers of black and brown children into urban schools, especially in London, the Midlands, West Yorkshire and Merseyside, from exotic parts of the world such as the Caribbean, the Indian sub-continent and East Africa, was creating problems for individual teachers and strains on local education authority resources. The question, then, was how best these newcomers could be absorbed into the English school system and the English way of life as quickly as possible and with the minimum of disruption to white children. The answer lay in the establishment of special classes/centres for teaching English to immigrants and the preparation of crash materials for teaching English to immigrant pupils. (DES, 1963, 1971, 1972). The underlying assumption was that, in time, these newcomers would become an integral part of British Society and would be assimilated into the British way of life. (HMSO, 1964; Watson, 1977; Kirp, 1979).

Almost twenty years later the question remains much the same. In the minds of many people the answer also remains very much the same, even though in reality schools are dealing less with large numbers of "immigrants" than with first or second generation coloured Britons who have been born in the UK. The underlying assumption that all would be well in the end and that assimilation or integration was just a matter of time, has, however, been rudely shattered. The riots in Bristol, Birmingham, Brixton and Liverpool destroyed many illusions. The subsequent reports into the state of race relations in the country merely reinforced what many had come to realise - that harmonious race relations do not just develop: they have to be worked at.

While the Rampton Report (HMSO, 1981a) was specifically concerned with the performance of West Indian pupils in schools and the Scarman Report (HMSO, 1981b) was concerned with race relations, employment and policing in Brixton, a rundown part of South London, both reports highlighted the underlying racism that affects this country, whether it is institutionalised in the power structures or amongst those who hold power or whether it is in subconcious attitudes of each one of us. Both reports pointed out that, as a result, there is a sense of injustice and resentment on the part of many West Indians and Asians living in this country, that in terms of housing, employment and educational opportunity and achievement, these "immigrant" groups are disadvantaged and that there should be positive discrimination in all areas of social policy and planning to help these groups.

This paper seeks to explore how far Britain is or has become multiracial, how far educational policies have exacerbated the difficulties of adjustment for both the host society and the immigrant communities, how other societies, especially in Western Europe, have coped with similar adjustments and what, if anything, can be learnt from a study of these societies´ approaches. In other words, "they might do it differently abroad", but do they do it better?

IS BRITAIN A MULTIRACIAL SOCIETY?

From time immemorial Britain has been a racial and cultural mixture. There is no such thing as "pure English" or even Anglo-Saxon, whatever the rhetoric of the National Front Party or even of the right wing of the Conservative Party may say. There have been waves of migration to and from these shores for centuries. Where the difference arises between recent patterns of migration and, say, those of previous centuries is in the scale of immigration to the United Kingdom in a relatively short time span (a matter of twenty-five to thirty years) of peoples with different skin colour, and different religions, cultural and liguistic backgrounds.

In the first major settlements there were Romans, Angles, Saxons, Danes, Normans, Jutes. Huguenots came fleeing from religious persecution in France in the sixteenth and seventeenth centuries; Jews came in the early part of the Middle Ages, until their expulsion in 1290. They came back again after 1656. They settled in even larger numbers at the turn of the twentieth century and in the 1930s. (And it should not be forgotten how much the Jews have enriched the life of British society.) There were refugees from Eastern Europe after the two World Wars. Spaniards settled in the 1930s, Greeks and Italians in the 1940s, Hungarians in the 1960s. More recently there have been other political refugees, most notably from Chile and from Vietnam. For the past two centuries there have been sizeable numbers of Irish and for much of this century sizeable numbers of citizens from the "White Commonwealth". Most of them have been absorbed or assimilated into British society without too much difficulty, largely because their numbers were relatively small. They were absorbed over a long period of time and by far the majority were of European stock.

After the 1950s, however, there was a marked change in patterns of immigration. Not only were the numbers arriving sizeable, but culturally, racially, religiously and frequently linguistically, they came from non-European stock. Which of these is the most difficult handicap for adjustment into British society is difficult to say, since each aspect can be a barrier in its own right. However, since there are so many myths and exaggerations made about the implications and consequences of these latest waves of migration it is worth examining some of them in order to establish the truth or otherwise of the claims made.

1. Numbers

The first aspect to be examined must relate to numbers. Because during the 1960s, and especially during the period 1967-73, when statistics were collected in schools(1) those classified as "immigrant" were either born overseas of had one or more parents who had been born overseas and had entered this country within a ten-year period prior to the statistical entry, large numbers who were born in the UK of "immigrant parentage" were not so classified even though they might have had considerable linguistic, cultural or religious adjustments to make. This difficulty was only partially resolved in the 1981 census.

However, put into perspective only about 5.5% (approx. 3 million) of the total population of the UK (56 million) are of immigrant stock or born overseas. While about 7% of all births are to women from the new Commonwealth countries, and, in a few places like Bradford, over 30% of all births are to Pakistani women and in Brent, Hackney and Haringay and several cities over 20% of births are to West Indian mothers, if one considers the population as a whole, coloured people account for about 2 million or about 4% of the total population of the country. Admittedly this is in marked contrast to the situation thirty years ago - in 1951 only 75,000 (0,02%) were of racial minority backgrounds - but does it make the UK a multiracial nation?

If one looks at Table 1 it can be seen that, in the larger perspective of immigration to this country, Irish, different

Table 1
Approximate Numbers of "Immigrant Stock" in the UK (1981)

Indians (including East African Sikhs)..................350,000
Pakistanis...250,000
Bangladeshis...120,000
West Indians...550,000
Chinese...20,000
Vietnamese..12,000
Africans...170,000
Irish..760,000
Germans..160,000
Americans..132,000
Poles..112,000
Australians/New Zealanders.............................100,000
Cypriots..75,000
Italians..60,000
Maltese...40,000

European nationalities and those from the old Commonwealth outnumber the "coloured" groups. Moreover, even allowing for some errors, on present predictions no more than 5% of the country's population will be non-white by A.D.2000. In the USA whose population is five times that of the UK 15% of the population is non-white. In Germany 9.5% of the labour force of twenty million who contribute to social insurance are migrants/immigrants, while in France the figure is 6.5%. Thus, in the context of immediate industrial societies (see Table 2) the UK can hardly be classified as nationally multiracial/cultural.

Table 2
Britain's Foreign Population in Perspective

Country		(1) Total Population (millions)	(2) Total from Overseas (millions)	% of (2) over (1)
Australia	(1978)	13.5	3.5	25
Canada	(1977)	22.0	6.0	27.2
			(.75m non-white)	
Belgium	(1976)	9.8	0.775	7.9
Britain	(1980)	56.0	3.0	5.4
France	(1978)	52.5	4.2	8.0
West Germany	(1980)	62.1	4.1	6.6

Sources: Various.

Moreover, over 45% of the black/brown Britons have been born in this country and can legally claim British nationality and citizenship. By the year 2000 between 65-70% are expected to have been born here.

In the context of the countries of South-East Asia, the Middle East, Africa or the Indian subcontinent (Corner, 1978; Megarry, 1981) the racial mixture and immigration of the United Kingdom is paltry, at least at the national level. However, at regional level, this is not the case and one of the issues that has caused so many educational headaches is that of uneven settlement. Thus, while coloured people might be very much "a minority" in numerical terms of a national basis, in many urban areas they are a very sizeable minority, and in many individual schools in the Inner London Education Authority, in Birmingham, Bradford, Ealing, Leicester, Leeds, Huddersfield, Walsall, Wolverhampton, Reading and Slough, they may actually form a majority of pupils. In all these areas over 20% of new immigrants at school are born to mothers from the new Commonwealth, while ILEA has 40% of its pupils who come from non-UK sources. Indeed in 1979 Sir Ashley Bramall, leader of ILEA, is reported as saying:

> "Inner London has 25% of the West Indian population of the whole country; in Spitalfields 40% of the population is Bengali and of 28 children taken into one primary school in the area in September, 23 knew no English at all; in one Church of England school in Soho 50% of the children are Chinese; and in North Kensington and Paddington hotel owners are recruiting Moroccans and Spaniards whose children arrive in schools without even the most rudimentary knowledge of urban life".

This picture can be repeated in many cities both here and in other countries affected by waves of immigration. Cities like Stuttgart, Cologne, Hamburg, Brussels, Stockholm, Gottenburg, Paris, Lyons and Marseiles are all very heavily settled with foreigners, migrants, settlers, gastarbeiter. Hamburg, for example, is now the third largest Turkish city in the world after Ankara and Istanbur. Los Angeles has the largest Vietnamese settlement outside Vietnam just as there are more Jews in New York than in the state of Israel. 37.9% of the population of Paris is foreign, 11.6% of Rhone-Alpes (Lyon) and 8.3% of Provence-Cote d'Azur (Marseilles) (Charlot, 1981) are the same. 25% of all schoolchildren in Melbourne, Australia, are from non-English speaking homes. (Taft and Cahill, 1981), while 25% of all children born in Sweden since 1978 are of immigrant parents. By the mid 1980s many cities in the USA (e.g. New York, Chicago, Philadelphia, St. Louis, Cleveland, Baltimore and New Orleans) will be over 50% non-white. Detroit and Washington D.C. are already over 80% non-white. The point is that in a wider international perspective the multiracial issues and problems faced in Britain fade into insignificance. No British city, with the exception of Bradford, has more than 12% of its people who are non-white. There are parts of cities which far exceed this figure, but on average the percentage of non-whites is far less than in many other cities of the world.

These settlement patterns pose particular problems for educationists. While it is possible to argue that the UK is not a multiracial society, compared with other societies, and while pupils in the majority of schools are unlikely to sit next to, let alone sit in the same classroom with coloured pupils, this is far from being the case in many inner city schools. It makes it hard to legislate for a national situation, therefore, when there are such regional variations and when those who carry on impervious to the changes that have taken place in our society can see no point in teaching their pupils about groups and issues which they are not likely to encounter. It is because there is no easy way of reconciling the position of those who believe that all children should be made aware of the multiracial dimensions of our society and those who believe that only those actively engaged in working in multiracial schools should receive support and guidance that it has been suggested that the British approach to the situation has been one of "doing good, by doing little". (Kirp).

2. Tolerant Attitudes

A second myth worth examining is that the British are a remarkably tolerant people. It is generally acknowledged that Australia has pursued racist policies with its "whites only/Asians out" policies of much of the twentieth century and that the American treatment of the blacks and the Indians is nothing short of scandalous and integration of schools through "bussing" could only be achieved by the use of federal troops. It is also widely accepted that the Canadian policy of Europeans (especially Anglo-Saxon) first approach, pursued until the 1960s, was basically immoral. The British scorn the French, who in any case tend to look down upon the North and West Africans and all who do not share the same ideals of French civilisation. To learn that the Germans are prejudiced against the newcomers, Ausländer, or Fremdenfeindlichkeit, should come as no surprise. Indeed terms of abuse such as "Kuemmeltuerke", "Spaghettifresser" or "Kameltreiber" are all too frequent. But the average Englishman believes that he is amongst the least prejudiced in the world. Being English is synonymous with being tolerant. But is it?

Milner (1975, 1983) showed that racial prejudice is deep seated in the British psyche. Jeffcoate (1979) and Rampton (1981a) give examples of more recent racism. All we need to do, however, is to go back in history to show how far we have progressed.

There have been coloured people in England since at least the sixteenth century. An act of 1531 was passed which outlawed "an outlandish people calling themselves Egyptians, using no craft nor feat of merchandise, who have come to this realm and gone from shire to shire and place to place, in great company and used great, subtle and crafty means to deceive people, bearing them in hand that they by palmistry could tell man's and woman's fortunes". The act was, of course, referring to gypsies, who could be hung without trial. Subsequent legislation, e.g. the Beggars Acts of 1536 and 1598, made similar reference to foreigners.

In 1601 Elizabeth I decreed that "the great number of Negroes and Moors who have crept into this land since the troubles between Her Majesty and the King of Spain" should be deported on the grounds that they were consuming food meant for Englishmen, although in reality the deportation order was a means of curbing vagrancy and unemployment. The North Africans of the late sixteen and early seventeenth centuries were made the scapegoats for the economic plight of Britain at that time just as much as "immigrants" are today.

There were large numbers of coloured people in England in the eighteenth century. In 1764 there were 20,000 negro servants in London alone, out of a total population of 676,250 (i.e. 2.9%), and during the century there were frequent petitions and protests against coloured people in Britain. For example in 1768 a bill was placed before Parliament designed "to prevent blacks being brought into the Kingdom". Yet at the time of the Napoleonic Wars an American visitor to London was so impressed by the easy-going relationship between blacks and whites that he saw fit to comment on it.

At the turn of this century there were riots in Cardiff against Chinese seamen and launderers, and in 1919 there were riots in Cardiff, Canning Town and Liverpool against the presence of negroes. Both periods of upheaval coincided with times of economic difficulty and unemployment.

The majority of immigrants were hardworking, law-abiding, and peaceful. A few, such as the negro John Richard Archer who was elected mayor of Battersea in 1913, even achieved political respectability.

It is as well to remind ourselves of the historical perspective, because racial intolerance runs deep in our history, has erupted in times of economic difficulty and social change, and because much of the present concern abour racism in this country voiced from many quarters is as much about deep rooted, institutionalised race as it is about superficial racial attitudes.

3. They have no right to be here

A third widely held belief is that immigrant peoples/migrant workers have no right to be here. It is often overlooked that they were frequently invited, sought political asylum or had rights of settlement because of the dual nationality awarded at the time of independence (e.g. to the East African Asians).

The reasons for migrating are many and various. Many who have come to the United Kingdom came because they were fleeing from persecution, war or political upheaval. This applied to Poles, Italians, Hungarians, Chileans, East African Sikhs, Vietnamese. Others came because they were invited, encouraged or financially induced to settle. This certainly applied to many Italian settlers in the brickfields of Bedfordshire or in the fruit industry of the Vale of Evesham. In 1950 London Transport began a massive recruitment campaign in Jamaica and other West Indian Islands for drivers, conductors and ticket collectors. During the late 1950s/early 1960s other employers began to recruit in Pakistan and India.

As early as 1946 James Callaghan was arguing in Parliament that labour shortages could only be met through immigration from the colonies. Other European politicians and labour leaders were thinking along the same lines and during the 1950s and 1960s bilateral agreements were signed accepting quotas of migrant workers from the poorer parts of Europe to work in the industrial societies. Thus the Swiss and German Governments signed agreements with the Turkish, Yugoslav and Greek Governments for quotas of migrant workers. In much the same way France welcomed in migrants from Spain, Portugal, North Africa and other French colonies. While many came as settlers, many entered on work permits of 2 to 4 years' duration. It has been suggested that the economic boom in France, Germany and Switzerland in the late 1950s, 1960s and early 1970s only occurred because of this large influx of cheap labour, exploited, badly housed, with no social security pensions or union rights and with limited security. In the absence of immigrant status migrant workers can be repatriated at the end of their work permit or can have their work permit rescinded early.

It is this area, particularly, that sets Continental Europe apart from the United Kingdom, because while the French, German, Swiss and Luxemburg authorities can simply refuse to renew work permits and can legitimately expel migrant workers within a few months - or days - if necessary, the British authorities are in no such position, whatever certain politicians may argue. How can a government "repatriate" citizens who are here on British passports, have been invited, have been given refugee status or who, increasingly, have been born here? Apart from creating a problem of "stateless citizenship" there are serious ethical implications in such an approach.

4. There have been coherent educational policies

The final myth to be exploded is that there is or has been a coherent policy towards new immigrants into this society. I have argued elsewhere (Watson, 1977; 1979; 1982; 1984) that the only policy consistently pursued has been one of laissez faire, allowing market forces to operate, as far as possible, without Government intervention. Government has not thought out the social or educational responses necessary for large scale immigration or settlement of racially and linguistically diverse groups in this country, although it was initially assumed that, through special English language classes, children of New Commonwealth parents would become assimilated or at least integrated into the "British way of life" as quickly as possible.

Because education is essentially a local matter in the British context, Government sought to pass the onus of responsibility for educational policy and provision on to local authorities. At no time has Government accepted that it has some responsibility for formulating national educational policies in response to the issues and dilemmas thrown up by their political - i.e. immigration - policies. Such a situation is not confined to the United Kingdom, but as one critic has observed "it is as well to remind ourselves that laissez faire is not the absence of policy so much as policy not to have a policy". (Nandy, 1971).

While in the 1960s the Government was content to allow individual local education authorities to formulate local policies, ranging from the establishment of special language centres, through withdrawal classes, to the integration of all children, regardless of race or religion, into the mainstream of school society as quickly as possible, it remained unashamedly integrationist. It saw the educational issues of the immigrant groups mainly in terms of language provision. During the 1970s the rhetoric changed from being integrationist to that of arguing in favour of developing a culturally plural society, without clearly defining what was/is meant by this term. Gradually, also, there has been a recognition that cultural pluralism has implications for the curriculum and for teacher education (DES, 1977; 1980; 1981) but short of issuing very generalised statements of intent successive governments have been unprepared to spell out what curriculum changes they envisage or how they see teacher education being changed. (Watson, 1984). The result is a measure of confusion on the part of practitioners and theorists. Since some of this confusion atises from misinterpretations of policy options it is to these that we should next turn.

POLICY OPTIONS

Once different ethnic groups find themselves in a nation state, whether through conquest, war, migration or boundary changes, the question arises of how to deal with them. (Watson, 1979). Does government policy in general, and educational policy in particular, seek to eliminate, modify or encourage cultural diversity? (Holmes, 1980). This is of vital importance since it will colour majority/minority and inter-ethnic perceptions.

Formal education in all societies is seen as a transmitter of knowledge, customs and social values. In culturally diverse societies, however, difficulties arise because a minority group (ethnic, linguistic or religious) may perceive the education system as providing or transmitting the cultural values of the majority group which it fears or which it rejects as subversive of its own culture, unless it can have access to its own educational provision. Such is the position with the Muslim minority in the United Kingdom.

In some societies the majority group (i.e. those holding power) may be prepared to allow a degree of cultural or educational autonomy for minority groups because it is politically expedient so to do, (e.g. in China, Pakistan, the USSR). In others, however, (e.g. France, Thailand) the majority find it most expedient to impose a common education, using a common language of instruction on all of its citizens. At the same time the curriculum and frequently the textbooks are centrally prescribed, on the grounds that such a policy is administratively more convenient and cost-effective and on the grounds that it encourages national unity.

The educational policies pursued depend on a whole range of interrelated factors, economic, administrative, cultural, social and religious. Ultimately, however, they depend upon the way the majority views its economic, political and/or cultural position vis-à-vis minority groups, and how minority groups view their position in society.

The terms majority/minority are not necessarily related to their numerical position in a given society. They are related to their relative political - and frequently economic - positions. (Hicks, 1981a). Thus in South Africa while blacks form a numerical majority they are undoubtedly politically, socially and economically inferior. They are treated by the whites as a minority. In Malaysia while the Chinese and Malays are almost equal numerically the Malays hold the political power and the Chinese the economic power, a delicate but not always racially harmonious balance. In the United Kingdom the Afro-Caribbean and Asian groups are numerically, as well as politically, economically and socially, minority groups. (Many would argue that the same position applies to the Scots and the Welsh.)

One is talking here about positions of inequality. A majority holds power, economically and politically; a minority is seen as inferior vis-à-vis the majority and is put in a position of subordination. Minority groups may or may not be easily set apart because of certain distinctive features such as dress, language, customs or religion. They may or may not feel threatened. They may wish to preserve their cultural identity or they may wish to integrate into the majority society, but where the preservation of cultural identity is seen as important, three aspects of this identity (religion, language and historical/cultural traditions) are seen as vital, if not sacrosanct. Some form of educational provision which preserves these three areas is eagerly sought. Some minorities are unhappy if they believe that the school system recognises and highlights their minority features, because they believe that this can lead to discrimination and prevent upward social mobility. There is growing concern amongst many groups in the USA that the policy of bilingualism is hampering the social integration and mobility of many ethnic groups, especially the Hispanics. Many Scots view the teaching of Gaelic as unnecessary and many Irish regard the teaching of Gaelic as anachronistic, while in many African countries education in native languages is likewise viewed as inferior to being taught in English or French because of the greater opportunities afforded by the international languages. Many minorities seek to integrate into the host society rather than stand out as something different. Thus many immigrants to the USA in the early part of this century eagerly sought integration as a means of social and economic mobility (Ravitch, 1976), just as today many West Indian parents in the UK are unhappy that their language is recognised as "different" because they believe that this sets them and their children apart from the mainstream of society. (Edwards, 1979; Stone, 1981). Many Asian settlers in the UK likewise wish their children to learn English rather than their mother tongue as the medium of instruction for similar reasons.

On the other hand there are those who fear a loss of identity if the school system does not recognise their religious and cultural identity. This has always been true of the Chinese wherever they have settled (e.g. Watson, 1976) and is true of many Muslim settlers in West Germany and England. (TES, 1983). If opportunities are made available, preferably with state support, for private or part-time education, whereby minority culture, languages and religion can be preserved (e.g. in Saturday schools or Koranic schools) (Stone; Krukowski, 1968) there is considerably less resistance to attendance at State schools, but the issue of different responses is extremely complex and has varied from one group to another in different circumstances and at different periods in history.

What, however, are the policy options open to governments? These range from extermination of minority groups (e.g. Jews in the Third Reich, tribal groups in Uganda, Buddhist hill tribes in Bangladesh); through expulsion (e.g. of Bangladeshies by the Burmese, of Chinese by the Vietnamese, of Asians by Ugandans), to separate development, whereby governments insist that different groups should live, be educated and have social intercourse in special reserved areas, usually inferior economically, climatically and/or geographically (e.g. the Indian reservations in the USA and Canada, the black homelands in South Africa and the aboriginal settlements in Australia).

While these are more general policies those with a direct bearing on educational provision are assimilation, adjustment, integration, synthesis and cultural pluralism. (Smolicz, 1981). What do each of these mean and how do they affect education?

Assimilation is the policy whereby immigrant groups or ethnic minority groups are absorbed, over a period of time, into the mainstream of majority society. They are expected to adopt the language, traditions, cultural modes and values of the host society. There is little, if any, recognition of different rights in law, education or social position. Schooling is used to good effect to ensure assimilation because not only does the curriculum ignore the different facets of minority groups, but there is an insistence at official level that teaching is through one language about one set of social values and customs. This has been the approach, whether explicitly stated or not, in the USA, especially towards Vietnamese (Kelly, 1981), in Canada, Australia, France and the UK until the 1970s. In fact the policy of the British Government in the 1960s and the early part of the 1970s was unashamedly assimilationist. In the mid-1980s many, if not most, teachers would hold this position. Many may use the terminology of multiculturalism but they really hope that the minority cultures will gradually disintegrate and be absorbed into the "British way of life".

Adjustment implies a process whereby immigrants are expected to "adjust" to their new society and new environment. They may make concessions but do not necessarily give up their cherished values.

A policy of integration differs from assimilation in degree. It implies a multicultural society up to a point, since the legal, religious, intellectual and cultural rights of different groups are legally recognised, but at the same time minority ethnic/immigrant groups are expected to integrate into the majority or host society. Such an approach is relatively easy where different groups are racially or religiously similar. For example, Vietnamese, Chinese and Khmers have been successfully integrated into Thai society as a first step towards assimilation. It has worked up to a point in Europe where different groups have settled in countries not their own, but it is increasingly apparent that certain groups, e.g. Lapps, Basques, Bretons, Catalans, Scots and Welsh have not been integrated into the host society, let alone assimilated into it.

A further approach is that of moving towards a synthesis, whereby all the different cultures and groups in a given society are welded together into some hybrid mix containing elements of them all. In time, theoretically, there will be a new, hybrid, culture. Individuals will identify not with their own ethnic group but with the new society being created. It is arguable that this was the pattern in the UK and most of Western Europe for centuries, until, more recently, new religious, racial and cultural elements were introduced. It was the aspiration of Lenin for the peoples of the Soviet Empire and of Mao for China's minority nationalities. The aim of the Malaysian rulers is to create a new Malaysian citizen whose primary loyalties are not to his Chinese, Malay or Tamil ethnic group but to a hybrid mixture of all, namely Malaysian.

More recently there has been considerable discussion about cultural pluralism. Roy Jenkins referred to this approach in the UK in the 1960s. Since the DES White Paper of 1977 (DES, 1977) it has become accepted jargon in official circles in the UK, but there is a decided lack of clarity over what is really meant.

The term was originally used by an American observer of the South-East Asian scene in the 1940s. J.S. Furnivall was particularly concerned about the effects of British rule in Burma and Dutch rule in Indonesia. (Furnivall, 1943). He described both these societies as plural societies where different ethnic groups lived side by side, meeting in the market place, but socially, intellectually and culturally never mixing. In truly culturally plural societies, such as India, Pakistan and, to some extent, Singapore, each group maintains its identity and has legal, educational and constitutional rights. There is a form of separatism within a framework of cultural pluralism but each group has equal rights and is equally respected. It could be argued that the United Kingdom (of English, Scots, Welsh and Northern Irish) traditionally operated within this framework, but there are distinctions within a culturally plural society which are frequently glossed over by politicians and theoreticians alike.

Does cultural pluralism imply separate but equal development for all groups or does it imply bi-or-multiculturalism, whereby each group is expected to learn the language and the culture of one or more than one other group within society? In the former case equal recognition is given to all groups with no attempt to enforce conformity to any one. In the latter cases both the dominant group and the smaller groups would be expected to learn each other's language and to learn something about their cultural and religious beliefs. The Australians, Canadians and Swedes are paying lipservice to and have legislated for biculturalism and bilingualism as the true measure of cultural pluralism.

What, however, about the position in the UK? It is easy to talk about a multicultural or a culturally plural society but what is really meant? What are the long-term implications? There is much vague talk about multiculturalism but it means different things to different people. Until there is some clarity injected into the debate, until there is some clear understanding about the type of society we are aiming at, the dilemmas and difficulties facing the education service are unlikely to be resolved because national policy will condition the policies pursued in schools. This can be most clearly seen by looking at other societies.

POLICIES AND PROVISION IN WESTERN EUROPE

Although it is recognised that many of the immigrant ethnic groups in Europe are only temporary settlers, migrants for a limited period of time, nevertheless they have to be adequately catered for and their children have to be adequately schooled. The supranational policies are therefore interesting because they recognise the educational dilemmas of preparing children (and adults) both for the host culture and also for a possible return to the country of origin.

The Council of Europe recommendation is that immigrant children or the children of migrant workers should be integrated into the host nation's education system as soon as possible, but that opportunities should be made available for instruction in the mother tongue and for children to be able to readjust to their home country should they wish to return home. Since 1968, and periodically renewed since, Council of Europe policy has been to recommend bilingual education.

The European Community likewise stresses the need for retaining the mother tongue, although until 1981 it never made clear whether this tuition was to be through regular classes in school time or in separate classes out of school time. Since April 1981, however, member countries have been expected to make provision for mother tongue teaching in ordinary classes, a position rejected by the Department of Education and Science for several years on the grounds that the ethnic minorities in the UK are immigrants, and therefore need English to get on in society, and are not migrants.

While the Belgian, French, Swiss and German Governments have talked about <u>integrating</u> the new ethnic groups into the school system - and society - as soon as possible, only Switzerland and some German states have made attempts to develop bilingual instruction extensively. The Swedish Government, on the other hand, has moved from a position of making statements about integration or assimilation to one where it is deeply committed to pursuing a policy of bilingualism and biculturalism.

Even so, it has been commented that "the salient feature of government policies everywhere (in Europe) is simply that there is <u>no</u> coherent general policy established by any government aiming at the legal, political, economic and cultural equalisation of the rights of immigrants. Instead one finds declarations of intent, and a number of uneven provisions in the fields of welfare and schooling...... In fact governments' paramount preoccupation has been the regulation of the

immigrant population......" (Giner and Salcedo, 1978).
How does policy operate in practice in individual countries?

France

The overall figures for the number of immigrants range from 3.4 million (6.5% of the population) to 4.2 million (8% of the population), although the overall number of children of school age born to foreign parents is only 7%. Until recently no official recognition was given to minorities although there is now a department especially responsible for monitoring their needs and progress. Although immigrants are generally expected to integrate into the French education system as quickly as possible since 1970 there have been a number of "introductory classes" for those needing special help in adjusting to the French way of doing things. There are about a thousand such classes throughout the country but it is reckoned that only about 2.3% of foreign children in French schools need any particular help. (Charlot, 1981).

Since 1978 there have been six centres established for the training of teachers of immigrant pupils, but it is generally believed that most problems occurring in school arise from socio-economic disadvantage rather than from linguistic or emotional difficulties. Moreover, the authorities are increasingly convinced that most families - and pupils - desire to integrate, through the use of French, as quickly as possible. Indeed many parents throw their hopes for a better life on to their children.

Nevertheless, since 1977 there has been increasing concern to provide classes in the mother tongue so that if necessary children can be prepared for a return to their home country if and when this arises. Such classes are for usually no more than three hours per week and are offered provided 20/25 pupils of the same nationality or language can be brought together for instruction. There is considerable opposition to this approach on the grounds that it creates uncertainty, both for the school authorities and for the children, because it hampers integration into the school system and yet is insufficient to foster the culture and language of the parents.

There has certainly been little official concern in France to combat racism in society or in schools through textbook revision or racial awareness courses for practising teachers. There has been little concern to teach about the backgrounds from which the children come. The opposite is more usually the case. Ethnic minority children should be integrated into the French education system and French society as quickly as possible through standardised curricula and textbooks and using the French language or they should be encouraged to leave the country as quickly as possible in order to ease the burden of unemployment and economic recession.

Educational Policy and Provision for a Multi-Cultural Society

West Germany

The German approach is quite distinctive. Germany does not regard itself as an immigrant country, even though many Turks and Yugpslavs clearly see themselves in that category. There is therefore no clearly defined policy of assimilation or of permanent integration. Instead, because most gastarbeiter are of European/Mediterranean stock and are there at the behest of Government or firms, education is viewed as much as preparation for a return home to the country of origin as it is for integration into German society. In 1982 the Federal Minister responsible for alien affairs said that:

> "German education policy for foreigners must be conceived with both integration and repatriation in mind. This calls for open-mindedness, understanding and the readiness to help on the part of Germans" (Bildung and Wissenschaft, 1982).

There are about 2.5 million migrant workers in Germany (or 4.5 million, including families). 45% of them come from Turkey alone. Most of the others come from Italy, Spain, Greece, Yugoslavia and Portugal, with whose Governments the German Government signed bilateral agreements allowing for quotas of workers to enter the country.

Most are employed in lowly, unskilled or "reject" jobs. There is considerable prejudice in housing and employment and most are regarded as second-class citizens. There is also increasing punitive financial pressure being brought against German firms that employ a disproportionate number of foreigners at the expense of German employees.

Throughout the German states there is concern for bi-lingual education, though there is variety in provision. In some states mother tongue teaching (in Turkish, Greek or Serbo Croat) takes place in regular school time, in some out of school hours, in others in the Turkish or Greek consulates. In some cases there have been experiments, with one nationality only learning alongside Germans, in others with mixed nationalities. The greatest success is where there is one linguistic group, since great stress is placed on the learning of German, which is regarded as vital for the successful integration of the workforce.

There is official concern, however, about the high failure rate in school. While 41% of foreigners who sit for the Abitur pass (cf. 82% of Germans), over 60% drop out or fail the nine years of compulsory schooling. The reasons given for poor integration into the school system are various:
1. prejudice and a sense of alienation on the part of the newcomer;
2. too many arrive too old to acquire sufficient German to benefit from the school system;

3. lack of linguistic skills because of insecurity, overcrowded classes, poor home backgrounds, inability to verbalise in class. There is a gradual acceptance that "real equality of opportunity can only be achieved primarily through using the mother tongue as the medium of instruction in addition to consistent teaching in German as a compulsory foreign language";
4. culture conflict between children and their parents. Which society do they belong to and for which are they being educated - German or Turkish or Yugoslav? Many children genuinely find themselves caught between two cultures;
5. inadequate teacher preparation.

The German authorities have been far more understanding of the difficulties facing their migrant workers/immigrant groups than have their French counterparts, but once again little practically is being done to counteract racial prejudice and many migrants complain about harassment on the part of fellow workers and police and immigration officials.

Sweden

Sweden is in an entirely different position since although 120 countries are represented in the immigrant figures (Ekstrand, 1981) over 60% of them come from the other Nordic countries and 50% are from Finland alone.

Although 25% of new births in Sweden since 1978 have been to foreign parents, 90% of the immigrant children in Swedish schools have been born in Sweden. Very few of them are coloured and it has been much easier for them to fit into the Swedish way of life.

Sweden has always set itself up as a model of harmonious race relations although in recent years there has been a backlash against the host nation on the part of many immigrant teenagers.

In the early 1970s there was a belief that after six weeks of intensive Swedish children of different ages could be integrated into Swedish classes. However the position has changed considerably during the 1970s and Sweden has now officially moved towards a policy of bilingualism and bi-culturalism, which means that not only is there recognition that six weeks is far too short a time to master the elements of the Swedish language, not only are immigrants expected to learn Swedish, understand aspects of Swedish society and at the same time preserve their own language, culture and customs but that Swedish children also are expected to learn about and respect the different cultures and customs represented by the immigrants.

There are special language classes for adults and children in groups as small as between three and five. There have been experiments with single language groups, mixed language groups, single language groups and Swedish children, mixed language groups and Swedish children. Research evidence would suggest that <u>one</u> language group, together with Swedish children, is the best means for achieving rapid integration.

However, there has been considerable professional and parental arguments about the policy of bilingualism. Many parents and teachers do not want bilingualism <u>within</u> school; if the mother tongue is to be taught this should be done <u>outside</u> school hours. Since 1977 the Swedish Government has provided financial assistance for mother tongue or home language teaching and for intensive Swedish classes and has been willing to provide teachers for both. Special teacher training courses to prepare teachers of Swedish as a foreign/second language have also been laid on. One hundred and sixty hours or tuition are given to both Swedish and other nationalities. Courses are also offered for the teaching of other languages such as Greek, Serbo-Croat, Danish, Spanish and Turkish, and it is possible within the comprehensive school system to take any of 53 different languages either as subjects or as second languages.

It is argued that because of this supportive approach there are very few emotional problems related to language difficulties amongst the immigrant groups, and also there are very low crime figures amongst first-generation teenagers. There is evidence also that, if parents attempt to become bilingual, this helps their children emotionally, socially and academically, whereas if they deny their old culture or try to preserve it at the expense of adjusting to life in Sweden, there are serious psychological effects on the children. In other words adjustment and integration while preserving a bilingual/bicultural approach are likely to be the most satisfactory in the long term.

WHAT CAN BE LEARNT?

What, then, can be learnt from these examples of "they do it differently abroad" in those areas of greatest concern in schools in the UK particularly as highlighted by the Rampton Report of 1981?

a) <u>Cultural adjustments.</u> While there are major difficulties of cultural adjustment in France and Germany, as well as in the UK, these are least noticeable in Sweden. This could be as a result of the Swedish Government´s bilingual/bicultural policy, but it is just as likely to be that the majority of immigrants (Finns and other Nordic peoples) have close affinities to Sweden and her way of life. Apart from a sympathetic and general awareness in the classroom situation on the part of teachers about the values, culture, customs and language difficulties of different groups there is little positive action that can be taken to ease the painful process of cultural adjustment. The position is infinitely easier the fewer the ethnic groups involved, but the classroom position can be eased considerably if parents are encouraged to take language classes as well. Perhaps we could learn from the French and the Swedes in this respect.

b) <u>Academic underachievement</u>. One of the major concerns in the UK has been over the academic underachievement of the West Indians in particular. As has been shown, however, there is similar anxiety expressed in Germany about the underachievement of Turks and Yugoslavs, and in France about those from North and West Africa. There is no easy solution because so many of the causes of underachievement are not necessarily connected with the education service, even though schools get the blame. However, as the Rampton Report points out, there are some facets which are associated ith education. These include racist attitudes, textbook bias, language instruction and inadequate teacher education.

c) <u>Racism/prejudice</u>. Much is made of this aspect in Rampton and in other reports and books of recent years. This is not the place to become engaged in this particular issue. The fact that such attitudes of prejudice and racism occur in all Western societies should not surprise us. Racism is endemic in the power structures of our societies and is particularly acute in France and West Germany. The Swedes (and the Canadians) are taking concerted action against racism. In the United Kingdom there is now greater awareness and recognition that racism exists. Gradually attitudes will be changed through textbook and curriculum reform.

d) <u>Textbook/curriculum reform</u>. The Rampton Report, the Schools Council (Little and Willey, 1981), Jeffcoate (1979), Hicks (1981b) and others have pointed out the bias and ethnocentricism of so many textbooks and syllabuses in use in schools today. Publishing companies and authors are slowly making amends, but with financial constraints many schools will continue to use existing materials rather than seek to purchase "better" materials. It is far easier, alas, to change things in centralized systems like Sweden and France, where the curriculum is officially prescribed or textbooks are officially "recognised", than is the case in a <u>laissez faire</u> system such as prevails in the UK, where individual heads and headteachers can make quite arbitrary decisions.

There is a danger that, as with sexism or peace studies, the pendulum may swing too far and books will seek to find racist overtones where none exist. Nor can the historical perspective be ignored. The slave trade did exist; Victorian attitudes to race and the mentality of colonial superiority cannot be denied; the economies of Third World countries have been, and continue to be exploited, but there is much in British history that deserves respect and acknowledgement.

Teachers can be - and must be - encouraged to redress the balance, but to do so without going overboard in the other direction. In Sweden and Canada there are courses designed to help teachers examine biased textbooks. There are also a number in the United Kingdom, but more could be done in this direction.

e) Language. Should bilingualism be encouraged or should all teaching take place through the host language? There is no clearcut evidence that would point in one direction rather than the other. Where children can learn in their mother tongue for part of their early schooling, where parents can be encouraged to be bilingual and to learn the host country's language and where mother tongue tuition can continue in the curriculum as a second language and as an examinable subject (e.g. why not Gujarati, Bengali and Punjabi instead of French or Spanish at O level/C.S.E?), the evidence from Sweden would indicate that children are likely to be psychologically, emotionally and academically well adjusted.

On the other hand the controversy surrounding bilingual education cannot be denied. On the continent of Europe most advocates of bilingualism are not the Asians, Turks, Yugoslavs or Moroccans. Instead they are the liberal-minded academics and policy-makers of the host nations concerned. The exceptions are some of the Muslim Asians who see mother tongue teaching as the best way of preserving their group identity. The same picture is true in the UK. At the same time there are many who believe, with some justification, that stress on bilingualism and mother tongue teaching will lead to continuing economic and academic inferiority on the part of the newcomers. Yet can it realistically be expected that mother tongue tuition can be provided throughout the school system if, say, twenty or thirty languages are represented in any given school? The expense, the difficulties of providing teachers, the value of the exercise, given the fact that children need English (or French or German) to progress in life, preclude this. It is possible that mother tongue teaching can and should be offered if sufficient parents demand it for their children, but provision can never be on such a lavish scale as that offered in Sweden.

f) Teacher education. Sweden, Canada, Holland and Australia are making considerable attempts to offer teacher education courses in second language teaching and in understanding the culture and background from which their ethnic pupils come. The German and Swedish Governments have allowed, even encouraged, foreign teachers into classrooms to undertake specialised work. A few local education authorities have done so in the United Kingdom, but there has been little clear guidance in this field. There has been even less guidance in the field of teacher education. Several recent surveys (Eggleston, et.al., 1981; Craft, 1981; Watson, 1984) would indicate that there is little emphasis on multicultural education for all students undertaking initial teacher training courses, let alone on in-service education for those actually working in the field. As for preparing teachers to teach Asian languages like Punjabi, Urdu, Bengali, Gujarati, Chinese or Vietnamese within the school system, this is at present non-existent. We have much to learn from Sweden in this respect.

Ultimately the key to improving race relations, developing new attitudes and either integrating newcomers into the host society or even developing a harmonious culturally plural society must be the teaching profession. This in turn depends upon adequate teacher education. In this field more than any other there is scope to learn from "how they do things abroad!"

NOTES

1.Statistics ceased to be collected because no use was made of them according to Margaret Thatcher who was the then Secretary of State for Education and Science. However, soon after returning to power as Conservative Prime Minister in 1979 she urged local education authorities to begin collecting statistics of different ethnic groups in their schools.

REFERENCES

Bildung und Wissenschaft (1982): Report on a speech made by the Minister for Alien Affairs.

Bhatnagar,J. (ed) (1981): Educating Immigrants, Croom Helm, London.

Charlot,M. (1981): The Education of Immigrant Children in France in Bhatnagar, ibid.

Corner,T. (ed) (1978): Education in Multicultural Societies. Proceedings of the British Comparative Education Society.

Craft,M. (ed) (1981): Teaching in a Multicultural Society: the task for teacher education, Falmer Press, Brighton.

Department of Education and Science (1963): English for Immigrants, DES. Pamphlet No. 43, London.

Department of Education and Science (1971): Educational Survey 13. The Education of Immigrants, London.

Department of Education and Science (1972): The Continuing Needs of Immigrants, London.

Department of Education and Science (1977): Education in Schools: a consultative document. Cmnd 6869. London, HMSO.

Edwards,V. (1979): The West Indian Language Issue in British Schools, Routledge and Kegan Paul, London.

Eggleston,J. et.al. (1981): In-service teacher education in a multicultural society, University of Keele, mimeo.

Ekstrang,L.H. (1981): Unpopular views on popular beliefs about immigrant children; contemporary practices and problems in Sweden, in Bhatnagar, op.cit.

Furnivall,J.S. (1943): Educational Progress in South East Asia, Institute of International Affairs, New York.

Giner,S. and Salcedo,J. (1978): Migrant Workers in European Social Structures in Giner,S. and Archer,M.S.: Contemporary Europe: Social Structures and Cultural Patterns, Routledge and Kegan Paul, London.

HMSO (1964): The Second Report by the Commonwealth Immigrants Advisory Council, Cmnd 2266, London.

HMSO (1981a): West Indian Children in Our Schools: the interim report of the Committee of inquiry into the education of ethnic minority groups. (The Rampton Report), London.

HMSO (1981b): The Brixton disorders, 10-12 April 1981. Report of an Inquiry by the Rt. Hon. Lord Scarman, O.B.E., London.

Hicks,D.W. (1981a): Minorities: A Teacher's Resource Book for the Multiethnic curriculum, Heinemann, London.

Hicks,D.W. (1981b): Two sides of the same coin - development education, multicultural education. New Era, 60, 2.

Holmes,B. (1980): Diversity and Unity in Education, Allen and Unwin, London.

Jeffcoate,R. (1979): Positive Image. Towards a multicultural curriculum, Chameleon Books, London.

Kelly,G.P. (1981): Contemporary American Policies and Practices in the Education of Immigrant Children in Bhatnagar, op.cit.

Kirp,D.L. (1979): Doing Good by doing little. University of California Press, Berkeley.

Krukowski,T. (1968): Canadian Private Ethnic Schools. Comparative Education, 4, 3.

Little,A. and Willey,R. (1981): Multi Ethnic Education: The Way Forward. Schools Council Pamphlet 18, London.

Megarry,J. et.al. (1981): Education of Minorities. World Yearbook of Education 1981. Kegan Page, London.

Milner,D. (1975): Racial Disadvantage in Britain, Penguin Books, Harmondsworth.

Milner,D. (1983): Children and Race: Ten Years On, Ward Lock Educational, London.

Nandy,D. (1971): in his forward to McNeal,J. and Rogers,M.: The Multiracial School, Penguin Books, Harmondsworth.

Ravitch,D. (1976): On the history of minority group education in the United States. Columbia Teachers' Record, 78, 2.

Smolicz,J.J. (1981): Culture, ethnicity and education: multiculturalism in a plural society in Megarry, op.cit.

Stone,M. (1981): The education of the black child in Britain: the myth of multiracial education, Fontana, London.

Taft,R. and Cahill,D. (1981): Education of Immigrants in Australia, in Bhatnagar, op.cit.

Watson,K. (1976): The Education of Racial Minorities in South East Asia with special reference to the Chinese, Compare, 6, 2.

Watson,K. (1977): Education for a Multiracial Britain: Some Problems and Possible Solutions. Paper presented to Third World Congress of Comparative Education Societies, London.

Watson,K. (1979): Educational Policies in Multiracial Societies, Comparative Education, 15, 1.

Watson,K. (1982): Educational Policies in a Multiracial Society, Spectrum, 14, 2.

Watson,K. (1984): Training Teachers in the United Kingdom for a Multiracial Society - the rhetoric and the reality. Journal of Multicultural and Multilingual Development, 5, 3.

Chapter Six

PREPARING FOR HEADSHIP AND SENIOR MANAGEMENT OF SCHOOLS

Derek Esp

INTRODUCTION

My interest in this subject began as a result of a three-month
journey through Europe in 1980 as the Association of Education
Committees´ Trust Fellow for the year. I am not a researcher,
nor have I been a headteacher, but I do have the doubtful
pedigree of being a bureaucrat. The knowledge on which my
observations are based stems from a look at headteacher
training in France, the Netherlands, Denmark, Sweden and Norway
and from involvement in organising conferences on this theme at
Gatwick with the Association of Teachers of European Education
and the National Association of Head Teachers. Current
involvement is with a project on school improvement co-
ordinated by the Organisation for Economic Co-operation and
Development. Although snippets of information from the work of
other people on what is happening in Spain, Germany, Belgium,
Italy, Austria, Switzerland, Japan, Australia, Canada and USA
are included in this paper, the emphasis of the examples given
come grom the five countries that I visited myself in some
depth as part of the AEC Trust Fellowship.(1)
    The general framework for the paper will be:

(a) General issues highlighted by my study;
(b) Some aspects of training in the five countries concerned;
(c) Some underlying problems and issues;
(d) A description of some international activities;
(e) Some agenda items in our search for better training that
    actually lead to improvement in schools.

    However, there needs to be a word of caution. It is the
view of this author at least that all descriptions of the
"state of the art" should have a health warning on them, in
that information is quickly outdated. The Belbenoit Report on
in-service training in the UK is one example of the way in
which an overview can quickly outdate.

1. SOME GENERAL ASPECTS

In any international comparison it is difficult to identify
what is national, truly international or dependent upon
individual initiatives. For example, in France I found a good
example of a negotiated training course which was entirely the
personal initiative of an "inspecteur d´academie". One general
feature, however, was the willingness of public authorities to
invest in training for school leadership. The UK now has at
least a "toe in the water" with the recent initiative announced
by the Secretary of State for Education and Science that there
should be special centres established for the regional training
of school principals.(2)

In the European schemes I examined it was interesting to
note the co-operation of researchers, teacher educators,
headteachers, teachers and advisers in course planning and in
training teams. There were few, if any, demarcation disputes.

Throughout the countries studied, courses seemed to have a
range of objectives, approaches, methods and "mixes" of
trainees. One key finding is the importance of objectives and
who sets them, though there is a general problem of evaluating
the effectiveness of training courses.

All the countries had in common the social pressures on
schools and the needs of school leaders. The common social
changes include participation by pupils, parents and employers,
dealing with financial crises, the problem of organisational
change, the impact of falling rolls, the rapidly changing
demands on the curriculum and the needs for curriculum
development and renewal. This does not imply, however, that
solutions can be universally applied. Individual responses may
be needed within each national or regional context.

There were some generally accepted training assumptions.
These are as follows:

(a) School leadership is no longer learned through experience
    or readily available through natural ability. There is a
    training requirement;
(b) School leaders require the skills of team leadership. This
    is vital if they are to cope with demands for
    participation, consultation and accountability;
(c) The school, (not the headteacher alone), is being given
    more autonomy in many countries. This in turn makes a
    demand for a different style of leadership.

2. AN EXAMINATION OF THE PROVISION IN THE COUNTRIES VISITED

My comments here will concentrate on the origins of training
programmes, their size and scope, their objectives and
emphases, the investment made in training programmes, the
nature of the trainers and attempts made at the evaluation of
training programmes. I have not attempted to deal with other

issues such as accreditation or the wider questions of planning and personnel policies. It must be emphasised, however, that the study made in 1980 did not at that time take account of other information that has since been made available, e.g. the extensive and rather different provision for teachers obtaining headships in French Catholic schools as opposed to those preparing for headship in State schools.

The Introduction of Training Programmes

In all five countries surveys by and pressures from headteachers have helped to establish the need for training, but very different circumstances have attended the introduction of training programmes. In France it was the events of 1968 that demonstrated the need for and, by 1970/71, the establishment of a national training programme for teachers who were being thrown in at the deep end as heads. In Sweden the "PLUS" Commission was established in 1972 to draw up a programme of school leader training. About the same time the SIA Commission on the inner workings of the school began its work. In 1976 two training programmes, one of them the school leader education programme, were established and funded for a 10-year period as an integral part of the SIA reforms which aimed to change the daily work methods of schools and develop their role in the community and give many local opportunities for decision-making and for the spread of "democratisation". Swedish educational developments were very different from those in Norway and Denmark. Norway developed training courses on a regional or county basis through various initiatives by national councils for education, while Denmark established a course for folkeskole heads in the Autumn of 1980 as a result of pressure from heads who wanted something "less academic" than courses provided in the past. In the Netherlands an enquiry by the headteachers´ association and the interest of the then Minister of Education established a national training course at Arnhem as early as 1976.

Training Programmes - Size and Scope

The size and scope of the training programmes are impressive. The French compulsory training programme has provided since 1974 a three-months long course in the April-June period for teachers who are taking up their first administrative appointment as head or deputy head in the following September. Teachers going to all levels of management responsibility and all types of secondary schools are trained together. The course comprises residential sessions where main themes are developed as well as periods of observation in schools, administrative agencies and private enterprises. The course provides a good grounding for teachers with little experience of school management. Short ten-day courses are provided for those with previous administrative experience and those designated as deputy heads in newly emerging comprehensive schools. In 1976 2,000 people were trained on the long and short courses. In 1980, following re-organisations, school mergers and the impact of falling rolls, 1,200 people were trained.

The compulsory Swedish training programme provides for all school leaders (heads and deputies) from all types of schools. Municipal school directors (chief education officers) and local politicians also take part. About 600 school leaders have been trained in each year since the courses began. To date (1983) some 400 out of the 1,200 "headmaster districts" in Sweden and half of the 4,500 school leaders have been trained.

In the Netherlands 1,770 people have attended the heavily over-subscribed course at Arnhem. Attendance on the course is voluntary, but the Ministry of Education pays all expenses. In 1979/80 a total of 550 heads and deputies from all types of secondary schools were trained. This training was extended to special schools from Autumn 1980.

Norway has provided training for many years, e.g. 18 of the 19 Norwegian counties provide training for their upper secondary school heads and training is generally available for heads of grundskolen (7-16 comprehensives). Other initiatives include a new course at Kristiansand at the Teacher Training College, which begins this Autumn.

In Denmark a new course, which began in 1980, provides 80 places a year for newly appointed heads of folkeskolen. Other courses in Denmark are provided by the headteachers' union and the main in-service training agency - the Royal Danish School of Educational Studies. A new course also began in 1980 for upper secondary school heads under Ministry of Education auspices. In all the countries visited heads were eager to participate in training programmes.

Who are the Trainers?

In France, the Netherlands and Sweden, a national training team is charged with the task of co-ordinating, developing and evaluating the training. In each case the trainers bring a wide variety of experiences.

The Dutch team, based at Arnhem, also organises the courses. This approach is appropriate in the Netherlands, where the country is small geographically and communications are good. In France and Sweden the central team of professional trainers provides a back-up service to regional teams. The 25 French regional teams ("equipes academiques de la vie scolaire") of from 12 to 30 or so in size, are all volunteers, many of them serving heads who undertake the training role in addition to their normal duties. An "inspecteur d'academie" is formally given the task of co-ordinating the work of the "equipe". In some cases a deputy "inspecteur d'academie" is given this task, and the time to do it, as part of his normal job. In Sweden the teams are led by a full-time trainer and his team members, many of them teachers, county inspectors and educational psychologists, who are on part-time secondment. In Sweden and the Netherlands the national teams have steering committees which enable the various interested parties, including teachers and local authorities, to be consulted on a regular basis. The combination of a central unit serving regional teams seems to work well.

If any particular "strengths" are to be singled out, then the French national agency, "Service de la Formation et de l'Administration" (SFA), has developed an excellent "bank" of case studies and catalogue of training methods and the Swedish team has done a great deal of work on evaluation of training programmes. Both centres give training, documentary support and an evaluation service to their regional teams. In Denmark the new course for folkeskole heads is based at the Kommunale Højskole (local government training centre) in Grenaa, which has already achieved a high reputation. The full-time number of staff running the course has teaching experience and will draw on help from the Danmark Laerer Højskole, the headteachers' union and some army psychologists. In Norway various initiatives are being taken by different national councils for education and by the Kristiansand Teacher Training College. What is striking, however, is the way in which information and experience are exchanged down well-established "informal grapevines" in Norway. There is also a trend for the various agencies to work together, e.g. the national councils for the comprehensive grundskolen and the upper secondary schools are planning a joint programme.

In all the training programmes there is an attempt to combine the experience and skills of full-time trainers and part-time practitioners who, in the words of an SFA trainer, can be "pragmatique".

Training Objectives and Emphasis

In content and emphasis the developments in Europe reflect the trends and functions from across the Atlantic. Initial attempts at training provided "administration" courses for heads, and then the emphasis changed to more general leadership, group work and human relations themes. There are signs of a stronger "administrative" emphasis in the French programme since SFA took over from its predecessor, INAS, and in all programmes there is an attempt to get a proper balance of administrative and human relations training. The greatest difference in approach stems from the degree of decision-making devolved to the school. In a system which provides detailed "rules" for the head the administrative training is prominent. This is so in Danish upper schools (gymnasia) whee a new course in 1980 concentrated on "administrative" problems for heads who have several volumes of regulations to understand. In contrast I encountered an excellent example of the organisational development approach in Norway in the County of Hordaland, near Bergen. This programme is based on ideas developed in the USA, the UK and elsewhere in Europe. The training of the head is an integral part of an organisational development programme for the school to which all the staff are committed. This course lasts three years and begins with a typical organisation and development analysis of the school which leads on to agreed priorities for development and innovation. The training of the headteacher takes place in the context of this programme, and in the last year schools begin to link together for contained mutual support as schools in contact (SIK). This programme makes massive demands on consultants running it, who require extensive training and are required in large numbers - 25 consultants are needed in Hordaland for the training programme and a further 15 to cover the work with "schools in contact" (all this for 200 grundskolen with between 3 and 50 teachers in each!)

Between the extremes of a "given" administrative training and the OD approach there are many variations. The Swedish programme puts its main emphasis on the work of the head and his deputy in "developing" their school and the success of the course depends on the degree to which the head does his homework and involves his staff. In the Netherlands the course encourages heads to meet in local non-residential sessions to consider school problems. It was interesting to note that the "long" course which I visited in France, which was run by the Academies of Nantes-Rennes, also put emphasis on the need for the head to "develop" the work team of all teachers and not only the formal leadership team.

Investment in Training

The resources put into training vary considerably. The Swedish course for school leaders is the largest, being a programme of 25 days over a period of two years and is divided into eight residential sessions of three/four days. To this must be added four weeks of "society orientated" practice. Substitutes are provided for heads for all these days, and in addition the head is given 10% of his working week or a half-day a week, to do his "homework" - the total investment amounts to the cost of the course plus 82.5 full days of substitution - more costly than a three-month residential management course! The French investment in training is also considerable, with over 20 days in residence and an average of two weeks of practical observation. In the Netherlands the course is recognised as a "survival kit" and the trainers are developing follow-up courses for those who have attended the initial 13-day course which provides for two periods of four days in residence. Whatever the variations for all these countries, training heads and deputies is considered worthy of a substantial investment.

The Danish course at Grenaa also provides for a basic course of
four residential periods totalling 21 days, plus three more
residential sessions over a total period of four years, whilst
in Norway provision has been reduced from four to eight weeks
in residence to a mere modest, but still substantial, 15-day
course for grundskole leaders and a "100 hours" course for
those in upper secondary schools. Length of course is important
if training is not only to improve the "performance" of the
head but to make changes in the schools which are seen as
beneficial by pupils, parents and teachers, and residential
sessions are considered an essential element by all the
trainers I met.

Evaluation of Programmes

Most training programmes have been evaluated traditionally,
i.e. participants and trainers have been asked by questionnaire
or in discussion to comment on the course itself. In Sweden and
France the total programme has been evaluated by an observer.
The real problem is evaluating the effect of the training on
the participants and their schools. Very little work is being
done on this aspect, except in Sweden where the school leader
education team at Linköping has just analysed the results of a
questionnaire to over 500 school leaders which indicates, even
with cautious interpretation, positive results in the schools.
(It also indicates that results are most positive where the
trainer adopted a more questioning and active guidance role
when helping the head to apply his training in the school.) The
Swedish team is now embarking on a five-year evaluation which
will look at a number of schools at the commencement of the
training course and again after two years and five years. The
work at Linköping could be of considerable help in moving
towards a more reliable form of evaluation.

I did not spend much time discussing the issues of
"qualifications" or "accreditations" for headship. All courses
were careful to avoid evaluation of the participant who needs
to be given confidence in his training to try improvements in
his own school and his own performance as school leader. The
one exception was a course at Kristiansand which gives
"credits", which will have salary implications, and provides a
"pass" or "fail". The course has been under heavy fire from
teachers' associations for this reason. Elsewhere this approach
is avoided: for example, in France training does not form part
of the teacher's assessment for inclusion on the "liste
d'aptitude" for promotion.

Trainers I met were keen to emphasis the needs of heads to
have a part in planning their own training. This is important
at strategic level when the course programme on offer is
planned, and at individual level. The Rennes Academie has
developed procedures for "negotiating" course content with
trainees, and in all the programmes which encourage

participants to initiate development programmes in their own schools there is an attempt to meet individual needs. Training programmes must have the flexibility to help the head to develop his own strengths and to allow his colleagues to assume leadership roles in the school. Training schemes have to be considered in the wider context of national and local frameworks and support structures. The most convincing training programme I saw was designed to meet the needs of individuals and schools within the context of a properly "orchestrated" support structure and framework. Ideally the rules, regulations, "personnel" policies, advisory services and systems of resource allocation should be designed and shaped as far as possible to accord with the objectives of "freedom of action" for the school team and its leadership.

3. SOME UNDERLYING PROBLEMS AND ISSUES

It is necessary to look at the wider context. Training by itself is too narrow a focus. We must also consider the context of canned and uncanned experience, selection procedures, staff appraisal schemes, job rotation, job enrichment, early retirement and other personnel policies. Otherwise we shall attempt to raise the dead or train the untrainable.

We have to look at the role of the headteacher and the school and the impact of legislation upon their role. Recent studies in the Netherlands have indicated that legislators must create the right conditions for schools to operate autonomously.

A further problem is the nature of leadership. What is it? Psychologists once outlined something around 1,200 qualities of leadership. We need to know more about what makes headteachers effective. Recent studies in the USA indicate that effective actions are often informal, small and unplanned.

We need to know more about the skills of leadership. Different contexts, schools and individuals may have different needs. We have to develop the idea of a training profile for potential leaders and for serving headteachers. In Canada, Leithwood of the Ontario Institute of Educational Studies has developed ideas about finding out what are the obstacles to leadership and helping people to obtain the skills to overcome these obstacles. In a conference in Germany in 1980, Clive Hopes listed some interesting development needs for institutional leaders. These are detailed below.

DEVELOPMENT NEEDS FOR INSTITUTIONAL LEADERS

(order in which the items appear has no significance)

TASK 1: EXAMPLES

1. Personnel Management

   - planning
   - recruitment
   - development
   - appraisal

   - experience in teachers in-service
   - management of professional and non-professional staff

2. Interpersonal Skills

   - communicating
   - motivating
   - counselling
   - handling conflict
   - committees and chairmanship

   - group behaviour
   - group leadership

3. Self-Management

   - managing stress
   - management of one's own time
   - self-awareness
   - self-development

95

4. <u>Institutional Planning</u>

   - assessing information from within and outside the school

   - forecasting trends and needs

   - determining policies and priorities

   - institutional evaluation (organising, reporting results, discussing results)

   - determining policies, goals and values

5. <u>Resource Management</u>

   - estimating

   - budgetary control

   - financial management

6. <u>Curriculum Skills</u>

   - development of curriculum

   - management of curriculum

7. <u>Management of Innovation</u>

   - creating innovations

   - reacting to innovations

   - responding to innovations

   - implementing

8. Organisational Skills

    - devising internal management structures

    - devising academic structures and record systems

    - allocating duties and tasks

    - understanding the school as an organisation

9. Relating to Governmental Systems

    - reporting to regulatory system

    - reporting to regional, state, national system

    - negotiating: with regulatory system
                   with other authorities

    - experience in the administration

10. Relating to the Local Environment

    - community

    - public relations

    - relation to professional groups

    - parents

    - church

    - local industry

    - culture

    - press

    - politicans

11. Knowledge of Laws

- law in relation to school

- personal rights

- youth and social laws

12. Educational Leadership

- supervision

- advising

- methodology

- discipline

- school events

13. Relating to Pupils/Students

- dealing with individuals and groups

- dealing with seriously disruptive

- dealing with seriously disturbed

14. School as a system in relation to other environmental systems

- system analysis

15. Developing a Philosophy of Headship

- role of the head

- styles of leadership

- awareness of values in relation to managing

- approaches to managing

Source: Extract from "Report on the Intervisitation Programme in the Federal Republic of Germany 1980" (edited Clive Hopes, European Forum on Educational Administration).

Another major area of difficulty is the unquantifiable nature of confidence, morale and motivation. I do not know how we begin to tackle the impact of factors such as these.

We need to know which training approaches meet which objectives best. School-based training has much to commend it, and overcomes some of the problems of training the individual outside of his/her own context. Even training teams together has problems, however, in that we can build a wall between the trained team and other members of the school staff. We need to learn from differing perceptions of the head's role and a new National Foundation for Education Research (NFER) study is tackling this particular issue.

Evaluation is a key problem. The Swedes have gone further in trying to evaluate what happens as a result of training, but they will readily admit that we do not know enough as yet to be sure of our findings.

4. INTERNATIONAL ACTIVITY

A whole range of organisations are involved in the study of this field - the European Economic Community, FIPESO Council of Europe, Association of Teachers of European Education, teacher associations, the European Forum of the British Educational Management and Administration Society, the Organisation for Economic Co-operation and Development. All have projects in hand and between them represent a massive potential "fire power". In all these international activities, however, it is important to involve more teachers in the various activities which often involve large numbers of researchers and administrators.

Task 3 (Results)

Are programmes offered to cover the professional development
needs of Principals/Heads?

```
(Principals/Heads only)        X = "well covered"
                               $ = "poorly covered"
                               * = seen as need but not covered
================================================================
I :x                          C   :B:F O:D D:E a  S:F:I:I:N:S:
T :  x                        O   :E:E F:E E:N n  C:R:S:T:E:W:
E :    x                      U   :L:D :N N G d  O:A:R:A:T:E:
M :       x                   N   :G:E :M M:L     T:N:A:L:H:D:
  :         x                 T   :I:R G:A A:A W  L:C:E:Y:E:E:
N :           N    x          R   :U:A E:R R:N A  A:E:L: :R:N:
U :           E       x       Y   :M:L R:K K:D L  N: : : :L: :
M :           E          x        : : M: : E      D: : : :A: :
B :           D             x     : :R A:1 2: S   : : : :N: :
E :                           x   : :E N: :       : : : :D: :
R :                               : :P Y: :       : : : :S: :
                                  : :   :   :     : : : : : :
1.:Personnel Management           :*: $ :$ *: X   X:X:*:X:$:X:
  :                               : :   :   :     : : : : : :
2.:Interpersonal Skills           :$: $ :X *: $   X:$:*:*:$:X:
  :                               : :   :   :     : : : : : :
3.:Self-management                :*: $ :X *: $   *:$:*:*:*:X:
  :                               : :   :   :     : : : : : :
4.:Institutional Planning         :*: $ :$ $: $   X:X: :*:*:X:
  :                               : :   :   :     : : : : : :
5.:Resource Management            :*: $ :$ *: $   X:X:*:$:*:$:
  :                               : :   :   :     : : : : : :
6.:Curriculum Skills              :$: * :$ $: X   X:$:*:*:$:X:
  :                               : :   :   :     : : : : : :
7.:Management of Innovation        :$: $ :X *: $   X:$: :*:$:X:
  :                               : :   :   :     : : : : : :
8.:Organisational Skills          :*: $ :X $: X   X:X:*:*:$:X:
  :                               : :   :   :     : : : : : :
9.:Relating to Governmental        :*: $ :X *: $   X:X: :$:*:*:
  :Systems                        : :   :   :     : : : : : :
  :                               : :   :   :     : : : : : :
10.:Relation to Local Environment  :*: $ :$ *: $   $:X:*:*:*:X:
  :                               : :   :   :     : : : : : :
11.:Knowledge of Laws             :*: $ :X $: $   $:$:*:*:*:$:
  :                               : :   :   :     : : : : : :
12.:Educational Leadership         :$: $ :X *: $   X:X:X:*:$:X:
  :                               : :   :   :     : : : : : :
13.:Relating to Pupils/Students    :$: $ :$ *: $   X:X:X:*:*:X:
  :                               : :   :   :     : : : : : :
14.:School as a system in relation :*: * :  : $    X:*:*:*:$:X:
  :to other environmental systems : :   :   :     : : : : : :
```

5. SOME AGENDA ITEMS FOR FUTURE ACTIVITY

First of all, there is a need to know more about what school leaders actually do that helps school improvement. The OECD tentative definition of school improvement is "positively valuable changes in student learning outcomes, in teacher skills and attitudes and in institutional functioning".

Likewise there is a need to know more about what hinders school improvement. Recent overviews by Mulhauser for the USA and Leithwood for Canada show how little we know about school leadership that is actually validated by research.

There is also a need to facilitate the exchange of trainers, so that best practices can be spread to both trainers and to school leaders.

In the OECD international school improvement project more information on the effectiveness of various leadership styles is being sought. Trainee objectives and methods are being studied and attempts are being made to find out what can be effectively assessed and evaluated.

Inevitably all this work cannot be tackled, at least not at once, but there is much that can be done. As in the case of training itself, it is important to have clear and validated objectives. As Drucker once said, "having lost our objectives, we redouble our efforts". It would be a pity to dissipate all the effort and resources available in this way.

Having outlined my preferred agenda, I recognise, like the Danish writer, Piet Hein, that "man is the animal that draws lines and then trips over them".

NOTES AND REFERENCES

1.Readers can find further information on the findings of this fellowship study in Esp,D.G. (1980): Selection and Training of secondary school senior staff: some European examples. Education, 17 October 1980; and Esp,D.G. (1982): The Training and professional development of school leaders in Europe. European Journal of Teacher Education, 5, 1-2.

2.Sir Keith Joseph, the current Secretary of State for Education and Science, recognising the need for school principals and leaders to receive in-service training, early in 1983 asked training institutions to offer their services for the training of headteachers. On the strength of the bids made, Sir Keith nominated certain centres, e.g. Bristol and Cambridge University Departments of Education, as regional centres for the co-ordination of in-service training.

Chapter Seven

CORPORAL PUNISHMENT IN SCHOOLS: ENGLAND AND WALES VERSUS THE REST?

Keith Watson

INTRODUCTION

One of the most persistent and controversial educational issues in English education is whether or not corporal punishment should be retained in our schools. Defendants of corporal punishment have argued over many years that its use in schools is dying out and that it is, in any case, only used as "a last resort" while opponents have argued that neither is the case. During the past decade there have been heated arguments between those who favour enforceable rules and values, with the cane being used as an ultimate deterrent for would-be offenders,(1) and between the Society of Teachers Opposed to Physical Punishment (STOPP) which has used the columns of <u>Education</u> as well as other publications to argue its case against.(2) The European Court's ruling in April 1978 in Tyrer v the UK (1977) that the birching of juveniles in the Isle of Man contravened Article III of the European Convention on Human Rights because it was "degrading treatment or punishment", the recent findings of the Scottish Council for Research in Education that abolition of corporal punishment does <u>not</u> lead to increased discipline problems in schools if handled correctly and gradually(3) and the subsequent decision to phase out corporal punishment from Scottish schools, the two cases ruled upon by the European Court of Human Rights in January 1982,(4) and the subsequent proposals by Sir Keith Joseph, Secretary of State for Education and Science, that parents should be given the right to refuse to allow their children to receive corporal punishment in schools, have all served to bring this issue very much to the fore once again. Never mind the fact that the 1982 European Court ruling was more about parental rights than about the inhumanity of corporal punishment; the media and STOPP perceived it as further ammunition in their campaign for complete abolition and a further 30 cases of children being "illegally" beaten are currently before the European Court.

Thus while corporal punishment is only one of many forms of punishment used in schools and while it is not as severe as suspension or expulsion, it can be much more brutal and inevitably it is an issue that excites the greatest controversy and causes great confusion in people's minds because the arguments used are often highly emotive(5) and because it is frequently suggested that England and Wales are out of step with all other "civilized" societies in legally retaining some form of corporal punishment in schools, even if it is not universally applicable. This chapter, therefore, is designed to take the reader through the current minefield of arguments surrounding corporal punishment in schools, to explore the philosophical justification for and the history of the abolition movement, to examine the legal niceties and the arguments for and against corporal punishment and to try to set the English situation in the wider international perspective, especially that of our European neighbours. At the outset, however, it is worth commenting that, to this author at least, the campaign launched by STOPP is misguided because it is frantically obsessed with abolition rather than with thinking out the implications of sudden abolition and with the need to introduce alternatives gradually.

PHILOSOPHICAL JUSTIFICATION

Deep-rooted in British educational thought and educational traditions are two major philosophical strands - Judaeo-Christianity and the thought of ancient Greece and Rome. From the former comes the retribution principle of "an eye for an eye..." and the much more important reformative principle of "spare the rod and spoil the child" (Pr.13:24) for "the rod and reproof give wisdom: but a child left to himself causes shame to his mother" (Pr.29:15). Proverbs 22:15 also comments that "Folly is bound up in the heart of a child but the rod of discipline will drive it far from him." These Biblical injunctions from the Book of Proverbs, which was generally accepted as an important treatise on education, applied as much to parents in the home as they did to teachers in the early Jewish schools, which were, to say the least, harsh places of learning. From Greece and Rome come the image of the flogging schoolmaster and the acceptance of harsh, even vindictive, forms of punishment used in schools through the ages in order to maintain order and discipline and to reform pupil misbehaviour. The likeness between punishment in Victorian schools and that meted out in Greek, Roman and Jewish schools is staggering.(6)

Perhaps the most important aspects of the Biblical teachings which are so frequently overlooked are the beliefs (i) that all punishment must be undertaken in a framework of love and the desire to benefit the victim; (ii) that punishment comes as a result of breaking the known parameters of behaviour; and (iii) that it should come within a "family relationship." Philip May in his book "Which Way to Teach?"(7)

103

shows that God laid down ground rules, order, a framework, in love, within which man could operate. When the rules were broken, punishment followed. The rules had to be enforced; the punishment had to fit the crime and had to be consistent; and the offender had to learn from his mistakes.

Unfortunately too many of the present day discipline problems, I would suggest, originate because there are no clearly laid down ground rules; too many parents and teachers do not believe in a framework or structure in which they and their charges should operate; nor do they state the rules and the punishments; nor, alas, are they often particularly demonstrative in their love. And without love punishment can become violent and abusive, especially where physical punishment is used. As Roger Ascham, Elizabeth I's tutor observed, "Love is fitter than fear and gentleness better than beating to bring up a child rightly in learning." It must be remembered, however, that most of the Biblical teachings on rewards, punishments and discipline (e.g. Pr.3:11-12; 6:23; 12:1; 13:24; 22:6 and 15; 23:13 and 14; 29:15 and 17) were aimed at parents. Difficulties have arisen where institutions, e.g. schools, have taken over parental responsibilities and duties. It is in this context in particular, as we shall see, that English schools and teachers stand out in marked contrast from their European counterparts.

All too frequently, however, discipline and punishment are confused. In school terms discipline is concerned with conforming to school rules, accepted patterns of behaviour, academic learning, etc., whereas punishment is much more specific and is concerned with a breach of these rules or codes of behaviour and

> "involves the intentional infliction of pain or of something unpleasant on someone who has committed such a breach of the rules. It must be inflicted by someone who is in authority and who has the right to act in this way."(8)

The major justifications for punishment are usually (a) that it should be Retributive - a mark of displeasure for an offence committed and a signal that such wrongdoing should not go unchecked; (b) it should act as a deterrent to discourage the offender or other would-be offenders from committing the same offence again; and (c) it should be reformative, designed to help the offender see the error of his ways so that he/she will not commit the same offence again. The advocates of corporal punishment in schools, as did their Roman, Athenian and Jewish predecessors, argue that caning (or tawsing) fulfils all three obligations. The opponents argue that the only true justification for corporal punishment is retribution, and that far from acting as a deterrent or as an instrument of reform it invariably has the opposite effect to the one desired.

HISTORICAL PERSPECTIVES

Although physical punishment in schools is still widespread there has been a steady decline in the severity and frequency of its use during the past two centuries.(9)

Dr. Johnson observed in 1775 that "there is now less flogging in our great schools that formerly" while the Clarendon Commission on nine public schools noted in 1861 that "corporal punishment has greatly diminished". In 1937 the NUT stated that "corporal punishment is rapidly disappearing from our schools" and as late as 1976 argued that "the use of corporal punishment in schools continues to diminish".(10) Nevertheless in that same year (1976) the National Children´s Bureau showed that corporal punishment was still used in 80% of Britain´s secondary schools.(11) This figure of 80% was further substantiated by STOPP in 1983.

In the past flogging in school was an accepted expedient for establishing good discipline.(12) For example, there was open rebellion at Eton, Winchester and Rugby over the brutality of the discipline and one rebellion at Winchester College, when the College building was held by mutinous schoolboys for two days, was only quelled when the militia had been called in and the ringleaders had been severely dealt with. John Keate, headmaster of Eton (1809-1834), earned himself the nickname "Flogger" when one day in 1832 at the age of sixty he personally flogged 80 boys out of a class of 198 boys in the upper school.(13) Next day he confessed to feeling rather tired. While the reforms of such heads as Thring of Uppingham and Arnold of Rugby lessened the brutality of the English public schools the right of prefects as well as of certain staf to cane or slipper malefactors persisted in many of the public schools and influenced attitudes in the grammar schools until growing opposition in the post-World War II period led to a review of the situation.

The history of attempts to have corporal punishment abolished in schools has been admirably told by Newell(14) but it is worth highlighting a few points because they reveal a significant shift in the body of opinion favouring abolition. As early as 1669 the so-called Children´s Petition appealing against corporal punishment was presented to the Speaker of Parliament and to several MPs "on behalf of the children of this nation".(15) Physical punishment was condemned by such figures as John Locke and Robert Owen and while attempts to have it abolished in the 1870s, following the 1870 Education Act, failed, at least measures to regulate its use and to ensure that the Head was ultimately responsible and that punishments were recorded in a book were gradually introduced.(16)

Changes in attitude towards corporal punishment have been gradual but nevertheless consistent. As a result of the Progressive Movement(17) and the recognition of the value of psychology as a distinct discipline in the inter-war years the Ministry of Education in 1938 sought the opinion of heads and teachers' organisations as to whether or not the law should be changed. The reaction at that time was negative. As a result the 1944 Act did nothing to attempt to control corporal punishment, and the report of the National Foundation for Educational Research (NFER) national survey, the first and only one of its kind, published in the early 1950s and subsequently criticised because of its inadequate research technique, concluded that not only was there overwhelming support amongst teachers for retention of the cane but that abolition would increase teachers' anxiety and undermine their already difficult position.(18) The then Conservative Government's views were that decisions about abolition should be left to LEAs and school authorities. This is still the official view held by the Conservatives, although it is proposed to allow parents the right to opt out of having their children beaten in schools. The Labour opposition on the other hand is committed to abolition legislation.

Apart from the polemical papers of the pressure group, STOPP, formed in 1968, there has been a growing body of opinion as well as research evidence during the 1960s and 1970s to substantiate the belief that the place of corporal punishment in schools should be seriously questioned, especially as it is no longer used in borstals, prisons or the armed forces. Some of the major official reports concerned with quite different aspects of education, e.g. Wakefield (1961), Newsom (1963), Plowden (1967), Pack (1977), have over a period of time come to oppose the use of corporal punishment in schools and to recommend alternative sanctions. The Plowden Report for example stated that:

> "the infliction of physical pain as a method of punishment in primary schools should be forbidden" and "the kind of relationship which ought to exist between teacher and child cannot be built up in an atmosphere in which the infliction of physical pain is regarded as a normal sanction".(19)

Subsequent studies have tended to reinforce these views. The study by Clegg and Megson in 1968(20), based on a study of 30 secondary schools in the old West Riding of Yorkshire, concluded that the use of corporal punishment did not reduce truancy or lead to better behaviour socially or academically, while Wright(21) showed that the effects of corporal punishment are transitory and the more severe the use of corporal punishment the greater are the inhibiting effects.

Other studies have shown that corporal punishment can lead to loss of self-esteem and to a lowering of moral standards,(22) that good attendance and absence of truancy are associated with low levels of corporal punishsment,(23) that praise is a far better measure of social and classroom control than severe or frequent punishment and that there are definite links between corporal punishment and vandalism.(24) Indeed Rutter´s important study of 1979 concluded that while it is hard to show a direct correlation between bad behaviour and a high incidence of corporal punishment there is a <u>tendency</u> for the two to be interlinked.

The British Psychological Society´s Working Party Report of 1980 suggested that, while not conclusive, there is considerable evidence to suggest that corporal punishment as a disciplinary measure is not only of doubtful value but is probably educationally harmful, especially if emotionally disturbed children are subject to corporal punishment and the underlying reasons why school rules are being broken are not examined. The Report concluded that:

> "After a careful survey and review of the relevant research literature, we can find no evidence which shows that corporal punishment is of value in classroom management. We have found evidence of its disadvantages although inevitably such evidence is not of the highest scientific rigour. Furthermore we consider its use to be indefensible on ethical grounds..."(25)

Attempts to introduce Parliamentary legislation to bring about abolition have so far proved unsuccessful. In December 1973 Baroness Wootton introduced the Protection of Minors´ Bill into the House of Lords and in January 1976 Denis Canovan MP introduced a Private Member´s Bill. Both were, not surprisingly, defeated, for judging by a recent survey of MPs´ attitudes to corporal punishment undertaken by STOPP, there is considerable indifference since only 106 (16.69%) of the 635 MPs issued with the questionnaire bothered to reply.(26)

THE LEGAL POSITION

While attitudes towards corporal punishment may have been changing the legal position has not changed in over 120 years. There has been no Parliamentary legislation concerning corporal punishment in schools, with the result that the legal position of corporal punishment in England is based on <u>common law</u> and the principle of the teacher acting <u>in loco parentis</u>, whereby the parent transfers his legal rights, including those of administering corporal punishment, to teachers in the schools via the LEAs. In effect the legal power to administer corporal punishment is vested in the LEA and is transferred to the head of a school or, in certain cases, to the deputy head, provided that a birch rod or cane is used and punishments are recorded in a punishment book. (Mansell v Griffin, 1908).

As Chief Justice Cockburn said in 1865, "A parent, when he

places his child with a schoolmaster, delegates to him all his, own authority so far as it is necessary for the welfare of the child". Such a view was upheld in 1929 by Chief Justice Hewart who ruled that by sending his son to school a father authorised the schoolmaster to administer reasonable punishment on the boy for breach of a "reasonable" school rule. As Barrell has shown,(27) the English Courts have consistently upheld the teacher's right to administer reasonable physical punishment and he cites numerous cases to support this position. One of the most famous legal cases was R v. Hopley (1860) in which a pupil in Hopley's care died as a result of excessive beating. In judging the case Chief Justice Cockburn said:

> "By the law of England a parent or schoolmaster (who for this purpose represents the parent and has the parental authority delegated to him) may, for the purpose of correcting what is evil in the child, inflict moderate and reasonable corporal punishment - always, however, with this condition: that it is moderate and reasonable.... A parent or schoolmaster who inflicts immoderate and unreasonable corporal punishment is answerable to the law and if death ensues it will be manslaughter".

In Ryan v. Fildes and others (1938) corporal punishment that included blows on the head, neck or ear were not considered reasonable and were illegal, but moderate use of the cane - 4 strokes on the hand (Gardiner v. Bygrave, 1889), 2 strokes on the buttocks (Ridley v. Little, 1960), the use of the flat side of a ruler (Mansell v. Griffin, 1908) and use of the tawse (McShane v. Paton, 1922) - are all regarded as "reasonable" and therefore legal. Slaps with the open hand or with a slipper, whether on the hand, leg or buttocks, would also be classified as legitimate corporal punishment but they would not usually be recorded in the punishment book as would caning or tawsing. Certain forms of punishment such as shaking, boxing ears, hitting on the head, beating with books or board rubbers are expressly forbidden.

However, there are three aspects of the law which are unclear in present circumstances.

(i) The principles of in loco parentis were enunciated before the enactment of the 1870 Education Act and subsequent legislation making education compulsory and date from the time when parents chose to send their children to fee paying schools and could withdraw them if they were unhappy or if they felt that the contract had been broken. The law has not reflected this fundamental change from optional (and fee paying) education to compulsory education, from the notion of a contract freely entered into by parents with a school or a tutor to one where the parent, by law, has to send his child to school.

(ii) Whereas it might be reasonable for a parent to hand over legal responsibility to a tutor or teacher of a small group, the modern teacher is not in a similar position to a parent since he has 20-40 children in his charge, with individual personalities and with the subsequent noise level and behaviour pressures.

(iii) While a parent has the right, under the 1944 Act, to withdraw a pupil from RE classes and from assemblies, he does not have the same right to withold delegation of his right to administer corporal punishment to the LEA or the school. Delegation of parental authority is automatic unless there is an agreement to the contrary. In Mansell v. Griffin (1908), for example, it was established that "in the absence of evidence to the contrary" the mere fact of sending a child to school implies that the parents have delegated their powers of discipline to the school authorities. While the 1944 Act (section 76) states that "pupils are to be educated in accordance with the wishes of the parents" the question as to whether or not LEAs should comply with parental requests not to delegate their rights of corporal punishment to that authority or school remains an open one. So far no English court has ruled on this issue but the ruling on the two cases before the European Court of Human Rights arguing that parents have the right not to delegate is likely to have important implications for both English and Scottish law, since the ruling argued that the British government was in contravention of Article 2 of Protocol 1 of the European Convention on Human Rights, which states that:

> "In the exercise of any functions which it assumes in relation to education and to teaching the State shall respect the rights of parents to ensure such education and teaching in conformity with their own religious and philosophical convictions".

As one STOPP pamphlet rightly observes "until the practice of corporal punishment in schools... is banned either by verdict of the European Court or by Parliamentary legislation, the law offers parents and pupils little defence against the teacher's 'professional' right to beat".(28)

The current position, however, is now one of some confusion. Since the European Court's 1982 ruling in favour of parents' rights to exempt their children from being caned Sir Keith Joseph has supported these rights, while at the same time he has refused to introduce abolition legislation, preferring to leave the decision to retain or abolish corporal punishment to the school governors of individual schools. Thus in July 1983 the DES issued a Consultative Document on Corporal Punishment in Schools which stated that "The Government proposes to introduce legislation which will oblige a maintained school to enable a parent to exempt a child from

corporal punishment..." It is expected that the enabling[/]
legislation will be introduced in the Autumn of 1984. This
will not be before a great deal of criticism has been made
and objections have been levelled at the proposals as
unworkable. Indeed it is ironical that Sir Keith has opted
for the very proposal that Lord MacKay, the Lord Advocate,
condemned as unworkable when he spoke before the European
Court at Strasbourg: "It would not be feasible," he said,
"to have a system in which children in the same class were
differently treated in this respect according to the views of
their parents because it must be fairly fundamental practice
of any reasonable system of discipline in a school, that it
should be seen to be fair....irrespective of their parents'
position, religion or philosophy." Already, rather than face
the difficult, and confusing choice of having to cope with
some children whose parents favour corporal punishment and at
the same time cope with others, in the same school, whose
parents oppose corporal punishment, many local education
authorities and individual head teachers have, not
surprisingly, opted for abolition.

DES Administrative Memorandum 531, Section 6 of 10 May
1956, stipulates that every school must record all cases of
corporal punishment in a punishment book. The head teacher is
responsible for its accuracy. It is subject to inspection by
governors or HMIs and it must be kept for three years after
it is full, though by whom is not stipulated.

However, there is not the same legal obligation on LEAs
to lay down detailed regulations concerning corporal
punishment. Section 33 of the 1944 Act suggests that LEAs
may make regulations, but there is no compulsion placed upon
them to do so. Newell(29) observed in 1972 that 25% of LEAs
in England and Wales had not drawn up or issued any
regulations, believing that the decisions were "best left to
the teachers".

Since local government reorganisation in 1974 the picture
is not dissimilar. By 1980, of the 104 LEAs in England and
Wales, 74 had drawn up regulations and 30 left matters to
the sole discretion of head teachers and/or governors (See
Table 1). There were, however, already a number of anomalies
because eight LEAs had yet to work out a co-ordinated
policy following on from reorganisation. Only 7 LEAs ensured
that every teacher had a copy of the corporal punishment
regulations.(30) The rest expected the head to inform the
staff what the regulations were. Even where there are
regulations these do not apply to the independent,
voluntary aided or church controlled schools. However,
because there is a considerable state of flux in many
authorities, it is difficult to ascertain an accurate
picture.

SCOTLAND

The position in Scotland is markedly different from that prevailing in the rest of the UK, partly because the different legal system and the different administrative structures have set it apart, partly because it has been decided to phase out corporal punishment and partly because hitherto the tawse or leather strap, available to all teachers and applied to the open palm of the hand, has been the most frequently used means of corporal punishment.

Corporal punishment in schools is an historic sanction in Scotland. It remained unaffected by the Children and Young Persons (Scotland) Act of 1937, Section 12 of which made it a statutory offence to assault a child or young person. The authority to use it is ultimately vested in the LEA, which should lay down regulations for its use and which de facto hands over responsibility to the head teacher. There is no legal requirement to keep a punishment book. However, it is not established in law that the teacher derives the right to use corporal punishment because he is in loco parentis. Instead the Scottish teacher has power under common law to impose discipline on pupils by means of corporal punishment. Until 1982 it was impossible for parents to deny the teacher this right, though if punishment is cruel or excessive the teacher can, as in England, be prosecuted for unreasonable behaviour.

Whereas in England there are statutory regulations governing the use of corporal punishment no such regulations exist in Scotland though the Scottish Education Deparment could introduce them if it so wished. Instead in 1968 it issued a Statement of Principles and Code of Practice governing corporal punishment which were drawn up by the Liaison Committee on Educational Matters, a now defunct body. While the ultimate aim was to see the elimination of corporal punishment and the recognition that "it should not be necessary in the modern primary school" it laid down minimum regulations to be followed (e.g. corporal punishment should not be administered for offences like latecoming or failure to do homework). In 1977 the SED went further and recommended that corporal punishment should not be inflicted on any pupil suffering from mental, emotional or physical handicap.

During the past decade there have been growing pressures to review the use of corporal punishment with a view to its eventual abolition. The Scottish Council for Civil Liberties has been actively campaigning against the strap, arguing that a slight shift in public opinion might persuade the Secretary of State to introduce abolition legislation. In 1972 the Edinburgh Education Committee´s decision to ban corporal punishment in primary and special schools was condemned by the Educational Institute of Scotland, the largest Scottish teachers association, yet far from condemning Lothian Regional Council´s Working Party (1977) "to hasten the elimination of corporal

punishment in schools in the Region..." the EIS itself voted in
favour of abolition in 1978. In 1977 the Scottish TUC added its
weight to the abolitionist lobby when it passed a resolution
calling upon the Secretary of State to phase out corporal
punishment in the primary schools forthwith and in the
secondary schools gradually, though the results of a survey on
pupil attitudes published the same year indicated that "two out
of three Scottish children favour the strap",(31) though how
far these views reflected the accepted custom and how far they
would change if abolition became possible is difficult to say.

Concern at the growth in truancy, vandalism, violence and
ill-discipline in Scottish schools led to the appointment of
the Pack Committee to look into their causes and to make
recommendations. While not specifically concerned with corporal
punishment the Pack Report nevertheless commented on it as one
of many sanctions and said:

> "While we do not dissent from the view held in
> several quarters that the sanction (of corporal
> punishment) should eventually be phased out, we are
> also very conscious of the fact that concomitant with
> this is the need to create a situation in which the
> use of corporal punishment to maintain order is
> unnecessary" and "We are of the opinion that corporal
> punishment should, as was envisaged in 1968,
> disappear by a process of gradual elimination rather
> than by legislation."(32)

More important, the Committee believed corporal punishment
was ineffective against delinquents and frequent truanters,
they believed it should be abolished in primary schools and
reviewed in secondary schools, that all teachers should be made
aware of the 1968 Statement of Principles and that LEAs should
formulate a clear policy on corporal punishment which should be
made known to all teachers in their employment.

The most recent study on corporal punishment in Scottish
schools, the SCRE Report "Making the Change"(33) found no more
than six or seven out of 400 Scottish secondary schools that
had abolished the strap, and studied 12 schools, 7 of which
used the strap and 4 of which had abandoned its use and a fifth
which was in the process of "making the change". It recognised
that "the profession is divided, even polarised, over the
question of abolition of the strap" because many believe there
is no alternative and many believe the consequences of
abolition would be disastrous.

The findings of the Report, however, should do much to
allay fears and suspicions. While agreeing that there is "no
one alternative" to corporal punishment the writers of the
Report show that alternative sanctions, especially methods of
reporting, referral, guidance and the involvement of parents,
have to be introduced gradually with the co-operation of and in

consultation with the whole staff and with clearly laid down guidelines. The Research showed that discipline was not any worse in schools where the tawse was abandoned, that good teaching ultimately depended on the calibre and personality of the teacher and above all that no teacher in an abolition school would wish to return to corporal punishment because they had better relations with pupils and the atmosphere in school was improved. The most significant aspects of the findings are that all the abolition schools involved worked very closely with the parents, that alternatives were clearly worked out and that good lines of management and communication were developed.

> While "there is no evidence that instant abolition of corporal punishment would be either desirable or successful or that the majority of Scottish parents and teachers consider it necessary"

the Report does nevertheless suggest that corporal punishment can be abolished provided it is gradual, an alternative system is developed and parents are made accountable for their children's behaviour. The debate is likely to continue, but the die has now been cast and corporal punishment will gradually become a thing of the past in Scottish schools, thus leaving England and Wales alone amongst the European nations in retaining it.

THE CONFLICTING ARGUMENTS

The Arguments for and against corporal punishment are many and varied. Space only allows a summary of the main arguments, but readers' attention is drawn to Table 2 and to the evidence submitted to the British Psychological Society's Working Party and to STOPP.(34) It is noticeable that the overwhelming support for the retention of corporal punishment still comes from the teaching profession which believes that decisions regarding its use should be left to the professional judgement of teachers, but even here there is now a wavering in the position of the diehards. The main arguments of the teachers' unions are that abolition would undermine the teachers' position, especially in areas where there is little chance of getting parental co-operation such as they could expect in Europe.

Since the 1960s there has been a polarisation between those who argue that corporal punishment is inhuman and degrading and those who argue that the moral and social decline of the country can be blamed on both the weakness of parents who have failed to discipline their children at home at an early age and on the "progressive", "pseudo-libertarian" ideas that have pervaded both schools and society.

The major arguments in favour of retention are that there is a need to maintain discipline in times of rapid social change, that without external discipline there can be no self-discipline, that, if a minority of pupils is allowed to undermine the position of the teacher and prevent other children from learning, LEAs are in direct contravention of their statutory obligation to secure "efficient education" in their areas, that it is supported and requested by the majority of parents and by the majority of teachers who fear that sudden abolition would undermine their position, would lead to chaos because of the indisciplined age in which we live, would be a vote of no confidence in the profession and would lead to the further erosion of respect for authority. Other arguments are that it is declining anyway, that it acts as a deterrent, that teachers are _in loco parentis_ and have to pick up from indifferent or weak parents who cannot or who have failed to discipline their children, that other sanctions are ineffective against certain pupils, that pupils prefer it to other sanctions (e.g. detention) because it is fair, just and speedy retribution and because it must be seen in the context of a "positive caring relationship between teacher and pupil".

The _opponents_ of corporal punishment argue that it is immoral, that it contravenes the European Convention of Human Rights, that it is degrading to both teacher and pupil, that it is ineffective as a deterrent, that it may contribute to or exacerbate poor teacher/pupil relationships, that it is a bad example because it institutionalises violence and encourages agression and vandalism, that it is logically incompatible with the idea of a community based upon mutual respect and care for the welfare and dignity of the individual, and its presence in schools may prevent teachers from seeking alternative methods of punishment, that it acts as a cover-up for weak and ineffective teachers, that it can bring about long-term psychological and sexual harm, (35) that it endorses the view that violence is permissible, that there is a direct correlation between the use of corporal punishment and vandalism, truancy and juvenile delinquency, especially in Scotland where the rates of delinquency, adult imprisonment and murder are particularly high and above all that it does not deal with the root causes of misbehaviour and ill-discipline.

The main criticisms, which have considerable validity, are that corporal punishment is not used as "a last resort". It is frequently used by a few teachers against a small number of pupils, that it is used against weak, handicapped and emotionally disturbed children, that it is used for offences which do not necessarily result from acts of direct disobedience or defiance and that the psychological research evidence shows that at best it is of doubtful validity, at worst it creates long-term, harmful effects.

Surprisingly, pupils are not averse to corporal punishment. In Scotland the 1977 SCRE inquiry into pupil attitudes to school rules and punishment showed that 67% of pupils agreed with the strap, though 50% would have preferred a better system. A similar survey carried out by the Irish Association for Curriculum Development in 1976 showed that over 50% preferred corporal punishment to sarcasm and other punishments, while 66% of girls preferred it to lines or detention. On the other hand the NUSS, representing an active minority bitterly opposed to corporal punishment, argues that it is not dying out, it is used frequently for relatively minor offences, it is degrading to both parties and it leads to student resentment, alienation and lack of co-operation.

THE INTERNATIONAL PERSPECTIVE

One of the major arguments used to justify abolition is that the majority of countries do not use it, even if legally approved, and that in Europe, the UK is the only country to allow its widespread use, especially now that Eire has finally banned corporal punishment in schools.

Interest in the international dimension is a long-standing one. A New Era survey conducted in 1929 covered 43 countries and found that in 14 it was illegal and not practised, in 9 it was illegal but was practised, in 7 it was legal and was practised and in 3 it was practised but not mentioned legally. More recent surveys would indicate an increasing number of nations that have abandoned the use of corporal punishment in schools (Table 3). While Scotland may be at one extreme and Sweden(36) may be at the other, most European countries would lie somewhere in between, with Poland having abolished corporal punishment as long ago as 1783 and Italy having never introduced it. Although it is officially banned in the Soviet Union the occasional smack and the humiliation of standing in the corner are not unknown while considerable pressures can be brought to bear upon parents of recalcitrant pupils by the State or upon pupils by their peers. Many would argue that psychological humiliation is more damaging than occasional corporal punishment. In the Scandinavian countries recalcitrant pupils may be suspended from schools more easily than in the UK, while in France, where pupil misbehaviour and disobedience are certainly not uncommon, the sanctions permisible are carefully detailed. These range from "a solemn warning" through several days´ suspension to an appearance before the disciplinary committee of the school. Failing the effectiveness of any of these, parents can be summoned to the school and if they still fail to carry out their responsibilities for disciplining their children, legal sanctions, including withdrawal of family allowances, may be undertaken. In Spain the Ministry of Education lays down detailed rules and regulations concerning the behaviour of teachers and pupils and strictly prohibits corporal punishment. The same is true in Italy. While the 11 German Länder (States) likewise forbid corporal punishment, at the same time the State authorities detail a code of conduct and permissible sanctions for school use on a step-by-step basis, which in Rhineland-Palatinate can, for example, ultimately lead to expulsion from all schools in the state.(37) As in France and Eastern Europe, the school cannot only call in the parents for a warning but can involve the State in bringing legal pressures against the parents where necessary.

While much is made of the European position by the abolitionists what is overlooked are certain fundamental differences between the Anglo-Saxon countries and the rest, especially in Europe. Firstly, as the Pack Report observed:

> "the legal powers of continental parents over their children..... are greater in exent than those available to Scottish (and English) parents and continental parents can be held liable for their children's misdeeds".

The European Court somehow overlooked this subtle but important distinction between the UK and other West European nations. Whereas legal responsibilities are placed upon parents for the disciplining and behaviour of their children in countries like Sweden, Germany and France, no such legal responsibilities are binding upon English (and Welsh) parents. Secondly, there is a major philosophical distinction between Britain and the Continent regarding the place of the school in educating children. In Britain teachers see themselves, and are seen, as "educators" concerned with pastoral care, character development, extra curricula activities of children, etc. as well as teachers of subjects. On the Continent of Europe teachers see themselves, and are seen, as first and foremost instructors, imparters of knowledge and skills without the pastoral and social responsibilities of their English counterparts. The latter responsibilities are largely left to parents, who are expected to be more actively involved in the educational process. This situation is changing in Sweden, and to some extent in France, but generally speaking it still holds true. Thirdly, education systems in Europe are conceived in national or, as in Germany, in State terms. The result is that there is a far greater degree of central control over administration, the curriculum, textbooks, examinations and, far more important, teachers are civil servants, subject to civil service rules, regulations, directives and security. They thus have behind them all the force of authority that the trappings of the State apparatus can provide. In Britain teachers are not civil servants, are not State representatives and cannot necessarily count on the support of the head teacher, let alone the LEA in any dispute involving themselves and the children in their charge. Teachers are appointed by the LEA, which to most people is an amorphous, ill-defined body, with few powers of sanction against ill-disciplined pupils. It is perhaps excusable that many English teachers feel exposed and cling to some form of punishment code as a means of enforcing their personal authority and it is not without significance that it is the teachers, through the professional organisations, who have wished to retain corporal punishment. It needs to be borne in mind that discipline and self-discipline begin at home. If parents cannot or will not control their children teachers see it as their responsibility to instill some respect for the rules of law, whatever methods they may use to do this.

The decentralised nature of British education is reflected not least in the different approaches to corporal punishment in the LEAs. As has been shown some have not even drawn up detailed regulations, while others have left decisions to the head teacher; some (e.g. ILEA, Brent, Haringay, Waltham Forest, Lothian and Strathclyde) have sought abolition at primary level, or at all levels, while others (e.g. Avon) reintroduced the use of corporal punishment in infant schools in 1976 for the first time since 1905, though it has since moved to an abolitionist position. Many LEAs, however, are reviewing their policy, as can be seen from Table 4.

CONCLUSION

While corporal punishment is the sanction that arouses the greatest interest and emotion and while there is mounting evidence in favour of abolition, it must be stressed that it is only one of a variety of sanctions which range from verbal rebuke, through extra work, detention, withdrawal of privileges, placing on report, referral, counselling, summoning the parents, reference to the governors, suspension, expulsion, transfer, and, if necessary, reference to the police and the courts. It is not as severe as many of these and its greatest merits are that it is quickly over and forgotten and that it can be specifically related to a particular offence. Positive alternatives need to be developed as replacements. These can range from changing the attitudes and ethos in a school, developing a guidance and counselling support system, giving misbehaving children greater trust and responsibility, to the development of special units or "sanctuaries". Until these alternatives are more widely developed and accepted corporal punishment is likely to persist, though it will dwindle slowly as LEAs strive to abolish it. Should Government legislation be introduced to ban the use of the cane or the strap, for example, under pressure from the European Court, more thought than is currently shown by the abolitionist lobby needs to be given to the legal position of teachers and of parents in England and Wales and there needs to be a greater understanding of the differences prevailing in the wider European position. Thus while it must be acknowledged that England and Wales are out of step with their European neighbours - even more so now that steps have been taken towards abolition in Eire and

Scotland - it must also be recognised that they are distinctive in many ways from their European partners and that any educational decision taken in isolation from their wider social ramifications, or taken hurriedly, as opposed to gradually, could prove short-sighted and could lead to unforeseen consequences. While we can learn from attitudes to corporal punishment abroad we need also to take into account the legal position of teachers and of parents. All might need to be changed together.

TABLE 1

Number of LEAs and Corporal Punishment Policies (1980)

	Number of LEAs	With Corporal Punishment Regulations	Headteacher's Discretion	Number of Corporal Punishment Policies
County Councils	47	38	17	55
Metropolitan Boroughs	36	24	17	41
London LEAs	21	18	3	21

8 LEAs: Berkshire, Doncaster, Gateshead, Gwynedd, Humberside, Rotherham, Tameside and Trafford - have yet to adopt a single corporal punishment policy following the 1974 re-organisation of local government.

Source: STOPP.

TABLE 2

Attitude to Corporal Punishment (1980)

Organisations opposed to the use of corporal punishment in schools

Advisory Centre for Education
Association of Directors of Social Services
Association of Educational Psychologists
Association of Metropolitan Authorities
British Association for Early Childhood Education
British Association of Social Workers
British Paediatric Association
Campaign for the Advancement of State Education
British Psychological Society
Free Church Federal Council
Howard League for Penal Reform
Institute for the Study and Treatment of Delinquency
MIND - National Association for Mental Health
National Confederation of Parent-Teacher Associations
National Consumer Council
National Council for Civil Liberties
National Union of School Students
Portia Trust
Royal College of Psychiatrists
Residential Care Association

Organisations in favour of retaining corporal punishment in schools

Assistant Masters Association
Association of County Councils
Headmasters' Association
General Synod Board of Education
National Association of Head Teachers
National Association of Schoolmasters/Union of Women Teachers
National Association of Social Workers in Education
National Union of Teachers

Organisations without strong views either way

Association of Assistant Mistresses
Association of Community Home Schools
Association of Head Mistresses
Association of Professional Advisers to Children's Regional Planning Committees
British Medical Association
Health Visitors Association
National Society for the Prevention of Cruelty to Children
Society of Education Officers

TABLE 3
Corporal Punishment: The International Perspective (1981)

Known Countries where it is still used in schools	Countries where it is illegal or it has been abolished dates given in brackets	
Australia	Austria (1870)	Portugal
Barbados	Belgium	Quatar
Canada	China (1950)	Spain
(Eire) (1)	Cyprus	Sweden (1958)
England & Wales	Denmark (1968)	Switzerland
(Greece) (2)	Ecuador	Thailand
Iran	Finland (1890)	USSR and the East European countries
Jamaica	France (1887)	
Libya	Holland (c1850)	West Germany
New Zealand	Iceland	
Nigeria	Israel	
Pakistan	Italy	
(Scotland) (3)	Japan	
South Africa	Jordan	
Saudi Arabia	Luxemburg (1845)	
Swaziland	Mauritius	
Trinidad & Tobago	Norway (1935)	
Turkey	Philippines	
United States (except for 2 states)	Poland (1783)	

(1) Eire finally abolished corporal punishment in 1982.
(2) Although it is officially illegal in Greek schools, many Greek students known to the author testify to its ongoing use.
(3) Scotland is in the process of gradual abolition.

TABLE 4

1. <u>LEAs which have abolished corporal punishment in all the schools under their control</u>. (By the end of 1983).

   Avon, Brent, Derbyshire, Doncaster, Haringay, Hounslow, Humberside, Inner London Education Authority, Lancashire, Leicestershire, Newham, Waltham Forest; Lothian and Strathclyde in Scotland.

2. <u>LEAs which have abolished corporal punishment for certain categories of pupil</u>.

   Buckinghamshire, Cheshire, Coventry, Gwynedd, Hampshire, Hillingdon, Kent, Kingston, Lincolnshire, Newcastle, Northumberland, Nottinghamshire, Sutton, Tameside, Trafford, Wiltshire.

3. <u>LEAs which provide regulations to all teachers</u>.

   Croydon, Liverpool, Wirral, Buckinghamshire, Oxfordshire.

4. <u>LEAs which are reviewing their corporal punishment policy with the possibility of abolition</u>.

   Enfield, Sutton, Gateshead, Berkshire, Dorset, Gloucestershire, Gywnedd, Lincolnshire, Nottinghamshire.

NOTES AND REFERENCES

Earlier and briefer drafts of this chapter first appeared as "Discipline and Punishment across Cultures", Spectrum, 1981, 13, 3; and as "Corporal Punishment in Schools", Education Digest, 1 January 1982.

1.Dr. Rhodes Boyson, Daily Telegraph, 21 October 1981; NAS/UWT: Discipline in Schools (1975) and The Retreat from Authority (1977).

2.STOPP: Corporal Punishment in Schools: The Unacceptable Face of British Education (1981); Corporal Punishment in Schools - The Abolition Handbook (1980); Corporal Punishment - Do Teachers know best? (1980); Peacey,N.: Corporal Punishment: a guide for concerned parents, Where 128, May 1977.

3.Cumming,C.E., Lowe,T., Tulips,J., and Wakeling,C. (1981): Making the Change: a study of the process of the abolition of corporal punishment. Hodder and Stoughton for the Scottish Council for Research in Education.

4.Both cases were brought by Scottish parents who believed that the LEA was acting illegally in not recognising their wish not to delegate powers of corporal punishment. In both cases the European Court found in favour of the parents. It did not, however, lay stress on the fact that parents also have responsibilities. See The Times Editorial, 26 February 1982.

5.STOPP (1981): A Quarter of a Million Beatings; STOPP (1983): Once every 19 Seconds.

6.Castle,E.B. (1961): Ancient Education and Today. Penguin Books; Allen,A.B. (1936): The Psychology of Punishments. Allman and Sons, London.

7.May, Philip (1981): Which Way to Teach? Inter-Varsity Press, Leicester.

8.Peters,R.S. (1966): Ethics and Education. Allen and Unwin, Hemel Hempstead.

9.Ryby,S.G. (1938): History of Corporal Punishment: Cambridge University Press; Gibson,L. (1978): The English Vice, Duckworth, London.

10.National Union of Teachers (1976): Discipline in Schools. NUT, London.

11.National Children's Bureau (1976): Britain's Sixteen Year Olds. NCB, London.

12.Barnard,H.C. (1963): A History of English Education. University of London Press. Sutherland,G. (1971): Elementary Education in the Nineteenth Century. Historical Association. Pamphlet G 76.

13.Lyte,M. (1875): A history of Eton College, cited in Barnard.

14.Newell,P. (ed) (1972): A Last Resort? Corporal Punishment in Schools. Penguin, Harmondsworth.

15.Freeman,C.B. (1966): The Children's Petition. British Journal of Educational Studies, 14, pp.216-223.

16.Maclure,S.: One Hundred Years of London Education, 1870-1970.

17.Watson,Keith (1980): The Growth of Progressive Education in the Twentieth Century. UCCF Associates, Leicester.

18.National Foundation for Educational Research (1952): A Survey of rewards and punishments in schools. NFER, Slough.

19.Plowden Report (1967): Children and their Primary Schools. HMSO.

20.Clegg,A. and Megson,B. (1968): Children in Distress. Penguin, Harmondsworth.

21.Wright,D. (1973): The Punishment of children in Turner,B. (ed): Discipline in Schools. Ward Lock Educational.

22.Aronsen,E. and Mettee,D.R. (1968): Dishonest behaviour as a function of differential levels of induced self-esteem. J. of Personality and Social Psychology. 9, pp.121-127.

23.Heal,K.H. (1978): Misbehaviour among school children: the role of the school in strategies for prevention. Policy and Politics, 6, pp.321-332.

24.Rutter,M. et.al. (1980): Fifteen thousand hours. Open Books, London.

25.British Psychological Society (1980): Report of a Working Party on Corporal Punishment in Schools. BPsS, Leicester.

26.STOPP (1981): Corporal Punishment. Views of Members of Parliament.

27.Barrell,G.R. (1970): Legal Cases for teachers. Methuen, London; (1966) Teachers and the Law. Methuen, London.

28.STOPP (1980): Abolition Handbook, op.cit.

29.Newell, op.cit.

30.ILEA, Buckinghamshire, Croydon, Oxfordshire, Liverpool, Newcastle, Wirral.

31.Pollock,G.J. et.al. (1977): Pupils' attitudes to school rules and punishments. Scottish Council for Research in Education report to the Educational Institute of Scotland.

32.Pack Report (1977): Truancy and indiscipline in schools in Scotland, Scottish Education Department. HMSO.

33.Cumming, et.al., op.cit.

34.British Psychological Society, op.cit.; STOPP (1980): Do Teachers Know Best? op.cit.

35.Gibson, op.cit.; British Psychological Society, op.cit.

36.In 1979 the Swedish Riksdag passed a law making it a criminal offence for a parent, let alone a teacher, to smack or strike a child from the age of 3 years upwards.

37.Newcombe,N. (1977): Europe at School. Methuen, London.

38.Watson,K. (1981): Discipline and punishment across cultures. Spectrum, 13, 3, pp.14-17.

WIDENER UNIVERSITY
WOLFGRAM
LIBRARY
CHESTER, PA.